In The Eternal 今

We Meet Again

intheeternal.com

Doi Tung, Thailand (2013)

In The Eternal 今

Book One

We Meet Again

Sara Chou

Seann Aswell

Strong Medicine Publishing

Montana

In The Eternal 今

We Meet Again

Strong Medicine Publishing
1001 S. Main Street #5231
Kalispell, Montana 59901
strongmedicinepublishing.com

Typeset using ConTEXt
Cover: Seann Aswell
Website: intheeternal.com
EU GPSR: strongmedicinepublishing.com/gpsr

ISBN 9798987382844 (ebook-Chinese)
ISBN 9798987382899 (paperback-Chinese)
ISBN 9798987382806 (ebook-English)
ISBN 9798987382820 (paperback-English)

Revision: ENPB-080825-01

To all of the brave souls who stubbornly persist,
despite resistance and adversity,
to do what they believe is right...

Know that you have probably done it before,
and you are not alone.

Contents

Authors Notes

This work depicts actual events in the life of the authors as truthfully as memory allows. All persons within are actual individuals, there are no composite characters. The names of some individuals have been changed or omitted to respect their privacy.

During consultations with Kevin Ryerson, the dialogue with Ahtun Re was recorded, and is presented in this book with his permission. Some portions have been omitted or condensed for brevity or clarity, for example phrases such as "Do you understand?" or "Do you follow?" after making important points, but otherwise the dialog is written as recorded.

Occasionally, dialogue between the authors may have originally occured at a different time or place, but all discussions presented actually happened. Most extended conversations between the authors were taken directly from recordings made at the time, and may have been edited for clarity.

All dream and visionary scenes are *Italicized* for clarity. Dates and locations are added where appropriate. All photos were taken by or for the authors, unless otherwise noted.

All editing has been done by the authors, who have engineering backgrounds, and are not professional writers. Therefore, there may be occasional updates and corrections to the electronic and print-on-demand versions of this text, which will be reflected in the version number.

This work was written without the use of any artificial intelligence (AI). However, AI has been utilized for marketing purposes.

The views and opinions expressed are the authors' own, and the information presented is for informational purposes only. Each person is unique, so please consult your own guidance or a trusted advisor, before accepting anything we say as being applicable to you or your life's circumstances.

TECHNICAL NOTES

This book contains Images and Photos, Notes related to people and Locations metioned, Book references, and Links to external resources, which are cited in the text and appear as references at the end of each Chapter.

All references include QR codes and URLs pointing to the book website, where more information about each item may be found. Links to external resources are first directed to the book website, to allow updating of stale links into the future.

Acknowledgments

We would like to give special thanks to Kevin Ryerson, who's work has allowed us to gain a deeper understanding of both ourselves, and the intuitively derived portions of the histories represented in this book. His unique ability as a trance channel, along with his wide range of knowledge and interests, has been an essential part of the process. (see Appendix B)

The work of Dr. Walter Semkiw helped tremendously in the early stages of our journey. His books, "Return of the Revolutionaries" and "Origin of the Soul", along with the case histories presented at his website, have provided much valuable perspective on the subject of past lives. (see Appendix B)

We would also like to thank Tom Kenyon, who's voice has been playing in the background for over a decade, helping our efforts tremendously.

And a special thanks to Joseph Knapp (Paramahansa Jagadish), who we met in Los Angeles at the start of our journey. His unique abilities, the result of decades of Yogic and Tibetan spiritual practice, helped clear our path forward.

Seann would also like to thank the resting soul of Hans Christian King. Each time we spoke, he would always ask, "Have you started that book yet?"

Preface

The University of California at Los Angeles[2] campus is located on the rolling hills of Westwood, just west of downtown LA. When visiting with friends in 1981, I was impressed with the beautiful sculpture garden, towering trees, and amazing architecture. Many of the buildings have their own unique characteristics; classical, modern, or artistic; but the one that surprised me the most was the boxy old engineering building.

My friend's office was on the third floor. I followed him into the building, and as we entered the elevator he pushed "3" but the elevator went down. I looked at him totally confused. "Aren't we going to the third floor?" I asked.

"Yeah!" He said with a broad smile, "Where we came into the building was the 5th floor."

My school, the University of California at Santa Barbara[3] is located right by the Pacific Ocean. The University Center is built on a slope that drops down to the water's edge gently. From the main floor, we could see the beautiful lagoon full of sea birds, and when looking past the lagoon at the blue ocean, white waves, one after another, breaking on the golden sandy beach with a perfect natural rhythm. From the balcony we could take steps down to the grassy area, then all we can see is the lagoon and the island in it. The view of the Pacific ocean in the distance is totally out of sight.

Those are pretty common designs for the structures built along side of the hills or on an ocean bluff. More than likely there are different entrances entering the building at different levels, and based on where we enter, we will have different vantage point of the surrounding landscape.

Often times, reading a book is like that. What we learn depends on our own level of comprehension. Like entering a building on a different level, we might come away with totally new understanding from reading the same book 10 years earlier, or 10 years later.

This book is written as stories and conversations with a similar intention in mind, hoping to provide readers with different entrances into this metaphorical building.

As those who work in computer software development know, every system has bugs. If we ignore the problem, it will get worse and worse until the whole system breaks down. In order to fix it, the first step is to recognize there's a problem. The second step, at least in my day, was to shut down the system and start the debugging procedure. Sometimes we need to repeat the measure several times to fully clear the bugs or glitches in the system.

Self-realization, or the progress of spiritual awakening, is very much the same. Through honest self reflection, and mindful practice with an open heart, we clear, heal, and let go of our past in order to free up space for new creations and new possibilities.

And, it's important to understand that some of those bugs we carry in our consciousness, may not just come from this lifetime, but may have originated in a previous life, possibly from many previous lifetimes.

The famous modern Chinese scholar, Nan Huai-Chin (南懷瑾)[4] was often quoted as saying, "If you just started to learn in this lifetime, it is too late!" Maybe, but a slow bird flying slowly is fine also. If we take reincarnation into consideration, life becomes a learning adventure and is part of a bigger blueprint.

When interviewed by the San Francisco Examiner in 1928, Henry Ford[5], founder of the Ford automobile company, said:

"I adopted the theory of Reincarnation when I was 26.... Work is futile if we cannot utilize the experience we collect in one life to the next. When I discovered Reincarnation it was as if I had found a universal plan.... Time is no longer limited. I was no longer a slave to the hands of the clock.... Genius is experience. Some seem to think that it is a gift or talent, but it is the fruit of long experience in many lives. Some are older souls than others, and so they know more... The discovery of Reincarnation put my mind at ease. I would like to communicate to others the calmness that this long view of life gives to me."

Reincarnation is commonly accepted in eastern religion and culture. More recently, much evidence has been uncovered by western researchers showing that reincarnation is part of many original texts that were compiled into what we now know as the Bible[6].

We may come into this world with a different purpose, mission, or experience, but our life experiences either from this lifetime or the past can provide what we need to learn in the way we need to learn it. For things we don't finish learning in this lifetime, we can continue in our next life. In other words, as long as we learn the lessons we need to learn, we can move on... That's how we progress, and in the process our perception of time expands.

Besides our story and personal experiences, most of the ideas or concepts illustrated in this book are not new. We believe we did our best to credit the authors or sources where they originated.

Belief, faith, and knowing is personal. What resonates with us may not be right for you. Choose wisely! Follow your own heart.

Sara Chou
Gabriola, BC, Canada
June, 2017

REFERENCES

1. [Photo]

   Gabriola (Gabriola Island, British Columbia)

   intheeternal.com/en/id/832

2. [Location]

   UCLA : University of California at Los Angeles

   intheeternal.com/en/id/423

3. [Location]

   UCSB : University of California at Santa Barbara

   intheeternal.com/en/id/424

4. [Link]

   Nan HuaiJin : Wikipedia page

   intheeternal.com/en/id/802

5. [Link]

   Henry Ford and Reincarnation : *The Henry Ford website*

   intheeternal.com/en/id/803

6. [Link]

   Reincarnation for Everyone (audio) : *Theosophical Society website*

   intheeternal.com/en/id/772

Introduction

Would you live your life differently if you knew that death was not the end, and that you will be born back into this world? That is not something I seriously considered until 2009, when I met Sara at a workshop in Albuquerque, New Mexico.

Over the previous several months I had shutdown my business, packed and put things in storage, preparing for a major life change. After that long weekend in Albuquerque, I was going to a remote cabin in North Carolina to write a book.

As we got to know each other over those couple of days (detailed in Chapter 13), it was clear that despite our differences, we had a deeper connection. In fact, I had never experienced that level of familiarity with anyone. While I didn't understand the significance of our meeting at the time, it seemed like a good start to the next chapter of my life.

A few weeks later, Sara sent an email saying we knew each other a little over 100 years ago, in China. In that lifetime she was a Concubine, and I was an Emperor. At the time I knew nothing about the story she told, but was open to the concept of reincarnation and decided to do some research rather than simply dismiss the idea.

It took a few months, but ultimately I had to accept that Sara was right. Understanding what that means, and integrating that awareness into my worldview, is an ongoing process.

HOW THIS ALL BEGAN

After we met in July of 2009, Sara started to remember. Flashes of revelation came first in the form of waking visions and dreams.

Then, events that had happened many years earlier started to make more sense, in light of her new insights. After a few weeks of processing it all she contacted me, telling the story of what happened on her drive back to California.

Many years earlier her Qigong teacher told her she had been Consort Zhen (aka: the Pearl Concubine). As a Chinese from Taiwan she knew the story well, but she was busy with her life as a mother of three daughters working in the technology industry, and did not have time or interest in entertaining that idea. However, after we met, memories came flooding into her consciousness that played like a movie on the screen of her mind.

Pearl - 1890's   Sara - 1970's

When she contacted me she expected closure, saying that she was glad I was doing well, and that she felt a sense of peace. Nonetheless, the exchange left me confused. How could she be so convinced that we had been these historical figures, and how could that be confirmed?

Having spent my career working with electronics, I had learned to balance intuitive ways of knowing with logic, so before accepting that I had been a notable historical figure in a previous life, I needed evidence. The fact that she had some visions, for me, was not enough.

A few days were spent reading what could be found online about those historical figures, and some of the stories seemed somewhat familiar, but what finally got my attention was a portrait. Most images of Guangxu found online in 2009 were artists renditions, few of which even looked alike, but I located a portrait by Charles Jacotin[10]. Pearl was known to have brought photographers into the Forbidden City, so it made sense that Jacotin would have had access to a photograph on which to base his portrait.

I purchased a high-resolution version from a French company selling licensed copies of Jacotin's work and sent it to my father, a photographer who worked in the printing industry, to get his feedback. He responded by sending a picture he had taken 10 years earlier from approximately the same angle, which is shown below.

Guangxu Emperor   Seann - 1999

The work of Dr. Walter Semkiw shows that physical resemblance does carry over from life to life, as the case histories presented on his website[12] clearly show. (also see Appendix B) Although I didn't discover Dr. Semkiw's work until later, the physical resemblance was compelling enough that I decided to take Sara's story seriously.

After locating a few books written in the early 1900s by someone who had lived in the Forbidden City, and who had extensive interaction with Guangxu, I had them express shipped. A few weeks later, inside the stained and worn cloth covers, the textured yellowed pages told a story which touched me so deeply that I cried. Maybe it was true. The timing and circumstances of how Sara and I met, the portrait by Jacotin, and now these books, containing first-hand accounts of interactions with a historical persona that looked like me, acted like me, and even had the same sense of humor as me, was too much to simply dismiss.

THE WORK

In The Eternal ⇔ is a trilogy, and is intended to illustrate that all of us share one thing in common. Our consciousness does not cease to exist when the physical body dies. We bring the essence of who we are with us into new lifetimes.

This book is an introduction to ourselves and how we came to learn about our journey thru time. Sara has had vivid recall of many experiences, much of which we have been able to confirm by studying the historical records as they exist in this time, by visiting some of the places we have lived before, and thru our consultations with Kevin Ryerson[13] (see Appendix B).

Some of the lifetimes we have explored with Kevin and have identified historically, will be covered in Book Two, Echos in the Halls of Eternity. As part of that process, we will be adding new perspectives on those historical figures and their stories. Book Three, We Are Here, will essentially be the book I originally intended to write, summarizing some of what we have learned on our journey thus far, while highlighting some practices and perspectives which may help you in your journey thru time.

OUR HOPE

The stories we tell ourselves about our lives and our world, deter-mine our experience. We hope that by sharing our story, we will help the reader better understand both themselves, and the larger reality we are operating within.

While our story is not unique, and we are not special, many Chinese consider the lives of Guangxu and Pearl to be a sad tragedy. However, by sharing what came before and after that lifetime, it's clear that in the big picture, we do have an opportunity to work thru our karma, and what may appear to be unfinished business. We will meet again.

Seann Aswell
Flathead County, Montana
August 2022

REFERENCES

7. [Photo]

Flathead (Flathead River, Montana)

intheeternal.com/en/id/833

8. [Note]

Pearl Concubine : About

intheeternal.com/en/id/502

9. [Photo]

Sara - 1970's (Taipei)

intheeternal.com/en/id/476

10. [Note]

Charles Jacotin

intheeternal.com/en/id/505

11. [Note]

Guangxu Emperor : About

intheeternal.com/en/id/504

12. [Link]

Reincarnation Research : Website

intheeternal.com/en/id/632

13. [Note]

Kevin Ryerson : About

intheeternal.com/en/id/589

1

Dreams

For thousands of years,
Lifetime after lifetime,
Immersed in a dream,
Intoxicating like a sweet wine.

— Author

It was before dawn, the world was still deep in sleep.
She slid out of her bed, carefully put on the black
traveling cloth, lightweight boots, wrapping cape and
hat; then took down the sword hanging from the
wall and walked down the stairs quietly. The
flickering lanterns swaying in the breeze, casting
shadows on the bushes in the garden. She skillfully
evaded the guards, quickly walking to the stable.

The first sound of rooster scratched the
silent night sky. The early rising birds are
jumping, dancing, swinging, and chirping
on the tree branches. In concert with the
roosters toiling to wake up the sleeping world.

She pulled out a black stallion, tapped and lifted
her hat a little, glanced at the dark, massive high
walls under grayish twilight for a second,
then leaped onto the stallion and sped away...

Nanjing, China
July 2012

I woke up and looked around our hotel room, remembering it was the morning of the 18th day of our visit in China. We had flown from Luoyang to Nanjing yesterday. As I sat up and grabbed the glass of water from the night stand, that clear image of the dream felt so vivid, hanging in front of my half opened eyes.

Over 20 years ago I bought a dream interpretation book from a new age bookstore in Malibu, California. The staff psychic told me, "In a dream, no matter who, where, or what happened, it is always about you, not anybody else."

"So just like the Enchanted Mirror, it should always be used to reflect on ourselves." I added jokingly.

"What do you mean?" She looked at me puzzled.

I explained briefly *Journey to the West*[15], the classic Chinese novel. One of the immortals in the story had an "Enchanted Mirror". When she would shine the mirror on any monster who pretended to be human, the original form of that monster would shown in the mirror. I continued to explain that Head Master Jih-Chang of the Bliss and Wisdom Buddhist community used to say, people who were newly exposed to Buddhist teaching often acted as if they received the "Enchanted Mirror". The problem is, instead of reflecting on themselves, most of them use it to shine at others. She laughed and said, "This master knows what he is talking about!"

Those years I was very interested in figuring out the meaning of dreams, and found a few interpretations that would sometimes work. For instance, when my sister shows up in my dreams, it's highly likely that I could get into fight or argument with someone. Dreaming about your father means you believe that your success and fortune is in your own hands. It also represents your courage in pursuit of the wisdom and knowledge. And dreaming of police means security, good future prospect, and stable life, etc.

Many years later, my partner Seann, who loves to burst my bubbles, said, "Those interpretations probably only apply to you. You believe them so they come true, like a self fulfilling prophecy."

Regardless, as Kevin Ryerson puts it, "Dreams are the language of the soul." Every dream, every night is unique. The dream world, no matter how confusing, how terrifying or how magical; can reveal the secrets buried deep inside our heart. Our most extraordinary dreams act like a mirror, reflecting our deepest desire, fear, struggle, and hope.

Sometimes dreams warn us of possible dangers, and some even predict the future. Often, the solution to something that we couldn't figure out when we were awake, is revealed clearly in our dreams.

The story of Zhuang Zhou dreaming of being a butterfly[16] is well known not just to Chinese, but is also well known to certain western scholars. Many different cultures believe some dreams are a message from God.

Therapist and sound healer Tom Kenyon[17] pointed out in a workshop that only about 15 percent of our dreams have special meaning, the other 85 percent are junk dreams, essentially just random background noise. Dreams, like meditation, can be used as tools to explore our inner self or subconscious mind, but we don't need to forcefully assign some special significance to them. In other words, look at dreams with both discernment and an open mind.

Sleep is the path to dream world. On average, we spend one-third of our life in sleep. By the time we are 60 years old, we have spent 20 years in sleep and about 8 years in dreams. Even though I became interested in dream interpretation many years ago, I started paying even more attention to dreams while in the PhD program at California Institute of Integral Studies[18], focusing on Transformative Studies.

One of the professors, an author and Jungian Psychologist, instructed us to keep a notebook and pen by the bed, and write down our dreams the moment we wake up. He suggested writing down everything as we remember it, without needing to understand the meaning or trying to make sense of the dream's landscape or timing. After about one month following the instructions closely, I suddenly grasped that I could be awake in my dream.

One morning, I dreamed that I was chased by two huge scary monsters. Just when I was running crazily for my life, terrified to the edge of my consciousness, I woke up in the dream and realized it was only a dream. So I stopped, turned around, faced at those monsters and said, "Wait! This is only a dream, you can't scare me. Go away!" They were stunned and like a deflated rubber toy, silently turned the other way and left.

"Ha! I got it!"

I woke myself up from the dream excitedly and wrote an email to my professor. The professor replied to my email with two words, "Dream on." After that experience, I could stay awake in my dreams more easily, and learned that the term "lucid dream" means just that. Many people have those experiences. To a Jungian Psychologist, they are not so unusual or special.

Of course, that doesn't mean that I am enlightened. Life continues forward, and at times old bad habits still unconsciously influence my daily routine. Even though I'm not in control of my dreams all of the time, it's much easier to be aware. And, it's easier to differentiate inspirational and prophetic dreams, or junk dreams that just showed up to help us process or clear our unconscious garbage.

One thing I came to understand over the years is that once we learn, experience, or realize something, it stays with us. Even though we may not consciously remember it all the time.

REFERENCES

14. [Photo]
     China Gate Tunnel (Nanjing, China)
     intheeternal.com/en/id/834

15. [Book]
     Cheng'en, W. (1550) *Journey to the West*
     intheeternal.com/en/id/813

16. [Link]
     Butterfly Dream : Wikipedia page
     intheeternal.com/en/id/770

17. [Link]
     Tom Kenyon : Website
     intheeternal.com/en/id/771

18. [Location]
     CIIS : California Institure of Integral Studies
     intheeternal.com/en/id/370

2

Mindlessness

*"Mindlessness is when our
thoughts and emotions aimlessly
wander, with no awareness."*

— Yongey Mingyur Rinpoche

Nanjing, China
July 2012

I put the glass of water down, crawled back into bed and tried to shake off my dream so I could continue sleeping.

"Hey" Seann turned over and tapped me on my shoulder, mumbling, "I don't want to be the 'wall', I want to be the 'pillar'."

"Ok, ok, you can be both!"

"Why?" He seemed woken up a little.

"Because you will be a much better 'wall' than me."

Happy with my answer, he turned and went back to sleep. But that brief exchange had disturbed my drowsiness and suddenly I found myself wide awake, reflecting on the dream I just had.

"In this place, at this time, does that dream have some special meaning?" I asked myself.

Yesterday we landed in Nanjing way past lunchtime. Seann had no interest in airport food, so we took a taxi to the hotel immediately. I was hungry and grumpy, still frustrated that we missed the delicious breakfast on our last morning at Christine, the hotel where we stayed in Luoyang, because he wanted to sleep late.

Christine - Breakfast

After looking around the room, he said, "Not as nice as Christine, but it's fine."

"It's a Sheraton, what could you have to complain about?"

"That's why I said it's fine." Then he added with a smile, "But I still like Christine more."

"Good, at least there's something you like about China."

"I like a lot of things about China," ignoring my unfriendly tone, he said thoughtfully, "like Shaolin Temple, Pingyao, the Lee Garden hotel in Beijing ..."

He could be so particular! As I laid in bed reflecting on our time in China thus far, I was becoming more and more disillusioned with our trip. Ever since we arrived in China, the culture shock stirred up a lot of discomfort in Seann and that created a lot of stress on me.

We landed in Beijing on July 2nd, and visited the Forbidden City three days later. I had been there 11 years earlier and really didn't like it, but it was an important place for Seann to visit. The whole place seemed super crowded, much more than my first visit, and the facility really didn't have the capacity to host that many visitors. Compared with the first visit, the energy and the environment had changed, and my dislike of the place exponentially increased. Even

Courtyard

though he was happy we went, other than Yang Xin Dian, Seann didn't like it either. We both agreed one day was enough, even though we didn't see everything.

Yang Xin Dian

Seann liked staying flexible, so I only booked Lee Garden before we arrived in Beijing, that way we could make adjustments to our plans depending on how things went. Once we left Beijing, the search for hotels became a regular part of my day. It was nice not being part of a prepackaged tour and on a fixed schedule, but it was also stressful for me.

After leaving Beijing we went to the Western Qing Tombs in Yi County, and spent a day exploring the Chongling tombs of Guangxu and Zhen Fei[23]. After spending some time alone in the tomb, Seann became a little emotional when he saw that people were making offerings to Guangxu, so we went for a walk.

We walked down an unpaved path toward the tombs dedicated to Zhen Fei and Jin Fei, which appeared to be visited less often, likely because it was off the main path. We were alone in public the whole time, which had rarely happened since arriving in China, making the peace and quiet even more enjoyable than usual. After soaking in the silence and reflecting on our day, we started the walk back to main path in front of Guangxu's tomb.

As we approached the tomb complex, there was a man offering horse back rides, and we couldn't refuse. It was Seann's first time to ride a horse, despite being from Texas, and our horses behaved very well on our ride down to the lake. That ride was the perfect ending to one of the more enjoyable days we had in China.

Seann's Horse Ride

Sara's Horse Ride

To get to San Zhi, our next stop, we had to take a sleeper train, which was also new for Seann. There were loud conversations in the hallway outside our door, the smell of smoke was frequent and strong, and it was a very uncomfortable bed. I was able to find a western style hotel once we arrived, so we were able to catch up on sleep before going to explore Taiyuan city and Chongshan Temple.

Chongshan Temple

Courtyard

While there we also took a tour to the 2800 years old ancient city Pingyao. Seann was enjoying the new and different culture. The environment was stimulating, but he had a lot of questions, and I was starting to feel a lot of stress.

Ancient City Tour

We had made it to Nanjing, but the journey had not been easy for me.

"Hey, I sense a disturbance in the force, what are you thinking?" Seann's head popped out of the comforter, aware that I wasn't sleeping and probably sensing my negative thoughts about him.

"I was thinking ... how annoying you are!"

He let out a deep sigh and was silent for a moment. "Remember what the monk said yesterday, that I am thoughtful and considerate, and I will take good care of you." He tapped the bed, "Please, sleep a little longer, there are many places we are going to visit today."

After a brief pause, noticing my motionless reaction, he continued, "You know, in order to be a 'pillar', you need good sleep!"

Just like that, he brushed away my unfriendly negativity.

China Gate

Yesterday, on top of China Gate, I was having conversation with a monk who graduated from the Chinese Buddhist College. While I was talking with him, Seann went to buy water, and when he came back was enthusiastically handling out cold water bottles to everyone, including the young boy who had been sweeping the floor.

"Is he American?" The boy asked.

"Yes."

"He is so handsome!" He looked at Seann with an admiring look on his face.

"He is kind and caring, a good-hearted person." I replied.

That was when the master monk looked at him and told me, "He is very thoughtful and considerate, attentive to details, a tender lover, a very good 'wall'. You have nothing to worry about, he will take good care of you. But you have to remember that, between two of you, you are the 'pillar'."

After the conversation, as we were walking outside Seann asked me, "What did the monk tell you?"

To avoid embarrassment, I only told him some of what he said.

After telling me I should be the pillar, Seann had fallen back into deep sleep, while I tossed and turned, not able to get back to sleep. My mind wandered up and down the path we had been on so far. The next day would be our 3rd anniversary, but at that moment, all I could think about were the arguments and disagreements. All the unhappy moments, related or unrelated negative thoughts, fettering and tethering, tighter and tighter, like a downward swirl, pulling me down, faster and faster....

An hour later the alarm went off, and woke Seann up.

"Ah, that was nice." He opened his eyes and looked at me smiling, and noticed I was wide awake. "Hey, did you sleep?" I kept silent, ignoring his question.

He turned the alarm off, "Are you angry at me again? What did I do? I was sleeping."

"It's okay." I shook my head and turned to the other side.

"Every time you get trapped in that emotional black hole," he sat up, "you only get dragged down deeper and deeper, and then get more and more angry, like there is nothing good about me. And then after the storm passes, you apologize and tell me that I am right."

"Not this time." I said, stubbornly.

"You say that every time." He paused a while, then changed the topic abruptly, "Remember 'Sara's way'?"

I was stunned and the speeding down the abyss was stopped. "Sara's way" was written while I was studying at CIIS (California Institute of Integral Studies). It was part of a paper I was writing while researching meditation practices.

"You forgot about it, right?" He said with a careful tone. "You know that if you focus on negative situations or emotions, you will only fall into the dark hole faster. No matter how I try to explain, it will only irritate you more. Only you can quiet your mind down, then choose a different perspective to get you out of that negativity. If you don't shift your focus, there's no outside power that can force you to."

"Sara's way" (see Appendix C), is based on that observation. The basic principle is, we attract the essence of whatever we focus on into our reality. So, when we dig deep into our consciousness and find a memory that brought us happiness, a moment that made us smile naturally, then we recognize the sensation we felt and hold that feeling. If we want peace and happiness, we need to focus on being happy and at peace. All the noise that our mind creates, prevents us from seeing the happiness we already have inside our heart.

Suddenly, I remembered being at the last CIIS retreat in Pacifica, seeing my eighty year old professor running down the hotel corridor hand in hand with his girlfriend, laughing like kids. When he saw me he slowed down and smiled timidly, and I smiled back at them, feeling their happiness.

Love! The most precious experience in life, forever desired by people through out time!

REFERENCES

19. [Photo]
Beijing Tourist (Forbidden City, China)
intheeternal.com/en/id/826

20. [Photo]
Christine Hotel Breakfast (Louyang, China)
intheeternal.com/en/id/453

21. [Photo]
Seann at Forbidden City (Forbidden City, China)
intheeternal.com/en/id/455

22. [Photo]
Yang Xin Dian (Forbidden City, China)
intheeternal.com/en/id/456

23. [Location]
Chongling Tombs, China
intheeternal.com/en/id/380

24. [Photo]
Seann's Horse (Chongling Tombs, China)
intheeternal.com/en/id/448

25. [Photo]
Sara's Horse (Chongling Tombs, China)
intheeternal.com/en/id/447

26.
[Photo]
Chongshan Temple (Chongshan Temple, Shanxi, China)
intheeternal.com/en/id/449

27.
[Photo]
Chongshan Courtyard (Chongshan Temple, Shanxi, China)
intheeternal.com/en/id/608

28.
[Photo]
Seann at Pingyao (Pingyao, Shanxi, China)
intheeternal.com/en/id/462

29.
[Photo]
China Gate (Nanjing, China)
intheeternal.com/en/id/445

3

Love

"...from the analysis of the life-work and
achievements of hundreds of men
of outstanding accomplishment,
there was the influence of a woman's
love behind nearly every one of them.
The emotion of love, in the human
heart and brain, creates a favorable
field of magnetic attraction, which
causes an influx of the higher and finer
vibrations which are afloat in the ether."

— Napoleon Hill, Think and Grow Rich

As a late boomer growing up in Taiwan, the emotional maturity of our college years was almost equivalent to today's high school students. Heavily influenced by the fairy tale like love stories written by a famous novelist, Qiong Yao, in our time, I was like so many young girls, singing,

"Life is precious,
Freedom is even more valuable,
But, for the sake of LOVE,
I can give up both!"

We were young and gullible, sensitive and emotional, full of imagination and fantasy, pursuing ideals that we couldn't fully understand. And, what we thought love was seemed to always be in hiding, only charging out of the shadows from a corner somewhere, knocking us out completely when we least expected.

After waking up, if we were lucky enough to wake up, we couldn't help but sing with a heavy sigh,

> "Gonna get off, gonna get,
> Have to get off from this ride...."
> – Dion Warwick's song from the movie "Valley of the Dolls"

Of course, life rarely follows our naive plans, and the search for what we believe love must be, often pushes us into uncomfortable territory.

In my studies I found no mention of "love" in traditional Chinese literature, nor in any of the many Buddhist Sutras I have read. Curiously, I asked many people why, but could not get a clear answer.

Love stories seemed to only exist in fairy tales, novels, and romantic poems. Why? Is it because for thousands of years, Chinese were conditioned to accept that survival is the only reality in life, and any other desire is just unrealistic luxury?

When I was young, I heard about an old lady who watched the movie *Liang Shanbo and Zhu Yingtai*[31] 107 times. Sad stories and movies seemed more popular with Chinese audiences, rather than stories of happy endings and hope. Inevitably, it became clear that I too carry what seemed to be a negative outlook towards life, seemingly entrenched deep in my soul, that I desperately wanted to break out of.

One sunny afternoon in the mid 1990's, I went to visit my Qigong teacher Jennifer in Malibu, California. She was renting an apartment from Shirley MacLaine[32], and when I arrived that afternoon she was giving Shirley Qigong lessons. After being introduced and sitting quietly in the corner for a few minutes, Shirley looked over at me and asked, "Are you going to sit there and watch?" I smiled and excused myself, then went for a walk on the beach.

I loved visiting Jennifer in Malibu, mainly because I loved the beach. One day while visiting, I saw Annette Benning, the beautiful wife of Shirley's brother, Warren Beatty, playing on the beach with their three adorable children. In high school, I was devastated after watching *Splendor in the Grass* and was angry that Warren's character abandoned his high school sweetheart, played by Natalie Wood.

My young idealistic self declared that I would never watch another one of his movies. On that beautiful afternoon, I remembered my childish behavior from many years earlier, and sent my best wishes to him and his family.

Nevada City, California
March 2012

For several months before we left California for our trip to China, we would go for long walks along the hilly back roads where we lived, and sometimes through the streets of nearby Nevada City. We were both a little out of shape, and knew we would be doing a lot of walking in China, so it was a good excuse to get outside on those beautiful spring afternoons.

Pearl on Shelf   Rock Shop

One day we stopped at a little rock and mineral shop in Nevada City, to see if they had anything interesting. Seann noticed an old postcard with picture of Pearl on a shelf, and asked the owner why it was there. Her answer was simple, "I just love that picture. She is so beautiful."

She didn't know much about Pearl, and we only told her she was a concubine, nothing more. But, it did seem like an interesting synchronicity right before our trip to China. When Seann saw that picture, I could feel it struck a chord, buried deep in his heart.

We planned to be in China for a couple of months, and were putting everything in storage and not renewing the lease on our rental house, so we wouldn't have to worry if we wanted to stay longer. One evening after our walk, Seann was cleaning out boxes of old files. He is not very photogenic, but his girlfriend was as beautiful as Natalie Wood.

That night, we had another long conversation, and he talked about his last girlfriend. When she hinted that she wanted to move in with him, he ended the relationship abruptly. After that short-lived relationship, having realized that he was not interested in marriage and family life, he focused his time and energy on his work and research.

I let out a long sigh...

What is love? How should we handle relationships?

One morning, during our coffee talk, I asked Seann, "What is love, really?"

"Love is just a word." He said with a quirky smile, "I think Alan Watts said that." I gave him a dirty look so he stopped smiling and got more serious. "I think love is an energy, something that isn't easy to describe."

"An energy?"

"It's the energetic exchange with people or animals. There are many kinds of love. For instance, maybe in one lifetime we could be brother and sister, and in another life we could be best friends, or fighting the same battle and willing to die for each other. Or, we could be romantically involved in one life and father and daughter in another. In all of those situations there is likely some sort of love, but how that energy expresses depends on the type of relationship."

"So, it's like a role play?"

"Kind of. The roles change, but the feeling of love and connection remains strong."

"What about relationships?" I asked, getting to the essence of my question.

"Relationships are about connections. Some come from biology, like the parental instinct to protect their children, something that we don't have option but to accept. But, maybe in another life your children are your friends or parents, and the way that love, or the energetic connection we call love, expresses differently."

That makes sense, in the context of reincarnation, but something was still missing. Then I found the quote from Viktor Frankl[35]:

> "Love is the only way to grasp another human being in the innermost core of his personality. No one can become fully aware of the very essence of another human being unless he loves him. By his love he is enabled to see the essential traits and features in the beloved person; and even more, he sees that which is potential in him, which is not yet actualized but yet ought to be actualized. Furthermore, by his love, the loving person enables the beloved person to actualize these potentialities. By making him aware of what he can be and of what he should become, he makes these potentialities come true."

A mother's love, or maybe a teacher's love could fit that description. But how common is it that a romantic love would rise to that level? My quest for the meaning of love continued.

One day, I said jokingly, "I wonder what Ahtun Re (one of the spirit guides Kevin Ryerson works with) would say about love." So during the next session, Seann asked.

After a long explanation, Ahtun Re summarized in one sentence. "Love is a self organizing energy field that sustains people through what appears to be the chaotic process of life."

I was speechless.

It's hard to imagine the power of the energy field generated by when two people are in love. Looking at it from that perspective, no wonder people and animals are stressed when they loose the love connection with their mate. There is an old famous Chinese poem,

> *Can someone in this world answer me, what is affection?*
> *That makes people (or animals) so*
> *committed and willing to die for each other.*

The original poem was describing a love story about two geese, but those two verses were widely used to describe love affairs, like Liang Shanbo and Zhu Yingtai, through out Chinese history. Suddenly, I realized that in Chinese culture and literature, "love" is more about material obsession and attachment, "affection" is actually the Chinese word that refers to emotional connections.

Unlike Seann, I had wanted children and a family. While my marriage did provide a family and children, I wasn't happy and felt that something was missing, so we ended up getting a divorce.

On a few occasions, in the early years after the divorce, my ex-husband asked if I would marry him again, suggesting that "I had changed", and that it might work out this time. I had changed, because I realized I was contributing to the problem. I had also learned that relationships are a two way street, and that problems will not go away just because we switch to a different partner.

Most conservative traditions encourage couples to work things out instead of getting a divorce. In today's modern society, divorce is more accepted. Therefore, when relationships present us with difficult lessons, many couples choose to go separate ways instead of staying together. Often times, facing and resolving core issues in a not so harmonious relationship takes a strong commitment, and much more effort.

No matter what we choose, whether we leave the unhappy situation for freedom, or stay in a less than ideal relationship for all the other reasons, the birds are still singing, the sun is still shining, and the world has not ended. We continue marching on, toward the unknown future.

And maybe, just maybe, when the time is right, while we are not looking, what we have been searching for all along...finds us.

REFERENCES

30. [Photo]
     Yuba River (Nevada County, California)
     intheeternal.com/en/id/825

31. [Link]
     Liang Shanbo and Zhu Yingtai : Myths and
     Legend website
     intheeternal.com/en/id/774

32. [Link]
     Shirley MacLaine : Website
     intheeternal.com/en/id/775

33. [Photo]

Pearl on a Shelf (Nevada City, California)

intheeternal.com/en/id/436

34. [Photo]

Crystal Rainbow (Nevada City, California)

intheeternal.com/en/id/440

35. [Link]

Viktor Frankl

intheeternal.com/en/id/776

4

By The Waterfall

The deep and innate love from
a previous lifetime, brought to
the present, and just like a dream,
we meet again, by the waterfall.

— Author

She slowed her stallion after prancing through
the valley for a long time. The sun was bright,
casting shadows through the branches of the trees,
dancing around her. Soft breeze caressing her
sweaty face, she stopped, glanced at the forest
surround her, could almost hear a babbling brook
somewhere near. Her stallion seemed understand
her thoughts, gathering smells with its nose in
the air, following with an exciting neigh,
then galloping toward the thick foliage ahead.

Emerging from the underbrush, there appeared a creek, her stallion slowed down, strolling along the rushing water. Waves of mountain wind blowing through the lush vale. The mist is getting thicker and sound of the water is getting louder. The rugged terrain with rock outcroppings from the bluff on the side of the creek was blocked by several giant boulders. She carefully rode the stallion around them and suddenly she found herself in a meadow. A breathtaking waterfall cascading down the cliff, roaring and splashing into the pond at the bottom of the fall. Colorful pebbles in the water reflecting sunshine creating rainbow sparkles all over the pond.

She got off the stallion, took of her hat, sauntered slowly toward the edge of the water. She bent down, and scooped some crystal clear spring water to wash away the sweat and dust on her face. The sweet scent of pine along with the cool mist from the waterfall floating in the air. She opened up her arms, standing on tip toes, took several deep breath, and whispered to herself the poem from Li Bai,

"Sunlit the incense burner, aglow in purple smoke, To afar, a waterfall drapes down like a shimmering curtain;"

She paused to appreciate the mesmerizing scenery.

"Rolling, flying, fluttering   plunging three thousand feet, As if it were the Milky way, hanging from Heaven."

A stranger's voice behind her completed the poem for her.

She quickly drew the sword out, turned and
pointed her sword in a defensive position.

Not far from her was an old pine tree, under
the tree was a stone table with two stone
stools. There was a Chinese chessboard, a
tea pot and two tea cups on the stone table.

"Hello my young friend, why
don't you join me for tea?"

A scholarly dressed person, with elegant and
gentle smile on his face, bathed in golden
sunlight, slowly walking toward her.....

Isn't that .... Seann?

Nanjing, China
July 2012

I jumped out of bed, suddenly waking from the dream.

"Ya, it's about time!" Seann sat in front of his laptop, "I was just thinking, if you don't wake up soon, I'm going to breakfast without you."

"Where did you come from, monster!" I bounced off the bed, went up to tickle him, "My friend would never leave me alone and go to eat breakfast by himself."

"Ok, ok" the ticklish Seann surrendered right away, "You win, you are the pillar!"

I smiled and went to the bathroom to get ready.

"I hope the head chef will be there today." He said.

"I know! I'm so hungry!"

Food is always a big issue when we are traveling. For many years it was difficult to find a good vegetarian restaurant outside of California. However, it's been even more difficult in China.

"But, can you compromise a little bit, we are traveling!" Sometimes I would confront him.

"Food is so important, how can we possibly compromise that?" He can come up with all kinds of justifications when he disagrees with me.

Environmental pollution, chemical pesticides and fertilizers, growth hormones, GMOs and artificial food additives...Seann is very conscious of it all, because of his time living on an organic farm. In recent years, I changed some of my bad eating habits because of Seann's constant nagging. Just quitting soft drinks and drinking more water helped me reduce the risk of getting diabetes. To prepare for the trip, we also did a cleansing detox program, eating mostly raw foods and exercising everyday.

"You don't know how lucky you are." He said.

"Right, in order to circumvent the possibility of being poisoned, we can just die of hunger." I said.

We had actually eaten a lot of good food, sometimes it just took a little effort. For example, yesterday at the hotel restaurant, I stared at the Chinese version of the menu and couldn't find a vegetarian dish. Just when I didn't know what to do, the head chef came over to the table.

His daughter is attending university in the US, and he heard from the waitstaff that there are Americans in the restaurant, so he came to greet us. After a brief chat, partly in English for Seann's benefit, he offered to make a vegetarian pizza for us.

As we walked into the hotel restaurant, the same waiter sat us down at our favorite window table and said, "I'll go inform the head chef you guys are here."

After brief chat with the chef, he told us he would bring us a surprise vegetarian breakfast. Seann looked vindicated.

"See how that works!" He said smiling.

"How what works?" I asked, knowing what he was about to say.

"When we are in a good place, things happen to help us on our path. Just like yesterday, you were stressed looking at the menu..." he said, tapping the table, "You were thinking our only options were a plain salad or cheese sticks, but I knew that we were going to have a good meal."

"And you knew that the chef was going to come help too?" I said, slightly irritated.

"No, but I was not surprised. It feels like it's another one of those days, where everything flows smoothly."

"Well, we are off to a good start." I said, sipping coffee and anticipating the chef's surprising breakfast.

REFERENCES

36. [Photo]
Waterfall (Pisgah National Forest)
intheeternal.com/en/id/468

5

Ancient City
Old Perceptions

*"Yesterday I was clever, so I wanted
to change the world. Today, I am
wise, so I am changing myself."*

— Rumi

Nanjing, the ancient capital of many Chinese dynasties, has been the focus of many legendary battles, with opposing forces fighting to gain control of the city. Crouching tiger, hidden dragon are the words typically used to describe its geological landscape.

Now, in modern times, high rises are popping up everywhere, with multiple lanes of congested freeways and ring roads encircling the old city, making it resemble many other large metropolitan areas. The mystical and enchanted scenery written about by famous Chinese poets throughout history are hardly seen anywhere, unless, I guess, you know where to look.

Our taxi made a wide turn and parked by the roadside. I regained conscious from my deep thoughts, and asked the Taxi driver, "Are we there?"

"You can walk from here, it's not far." He replied dismissively.

Seann grabbed his computer bag, ready to get out of the car. I tapped him, "Wait!" then turned to the driver, "We are going to Ming Xiaoling[38], that was the deal!"

Nanjing

"Ming Xiao Ling is right there!" The driver pointed to the hills, saying with an impatient tone, "It's very inconvenient for me to get out if I drive in there. You can walk."

I wanted to continue arguing with the taxi driver, but Seann gave the driver a one-hundred RMB bill, got out of the car and started walking.

"Hey, wait for the change!" I got out of the taxi, shouting at Seann. He ignored me and kept walking.

"Fine!" I thought, and slammed the taxi door, "Let's not get the change!"

I slowly approached the entrance at the end of a long walking path. My legs were as heavy as stone, barely able to move any further after the strenuous uphill walk. Seann was already at the entrance holding two tickets, with a young woman standing next to him, waiting for me.

"I told you we should not get into that taxi." He looked at me, and tried to smile, "Don't be angry. I am not angry at him anymore."

I wanted to yell at him but that young woman was there so I swallowed my anger.

"Can you ask her?" Seann pointed to the young woman, "Why does she keep following me?"

"Da jie (Chinese for elder sister), it's like this," the young woman turned to me, "I asked him if he needs a car," she pointed to an eight-seater golf cart. "I saw he bought two tickets so I told him, two for one hundred (RMB). He gave me one hundred and left, so I had to follow him."

I broke into laughter, "Privacy is very important to Americans. You stand too close to him. He didn't really understand what you were talking about. The one hundred he gave you was probably hoping you would leave him alone."

She heard my explanation, and quickly moved toward me. I stepped back a couple of steps unconsciously.

"So, let's go ride the cart then." I said, trying to ease the tension.

Seann jumped on to the driver seat of the golf cart, tapped the front seat and said to me with a delightful smile, "Come on, this will be fun!"

"Wait!" the young woman ran briskly to the cart, "That's my seat."

Ming Tombs Tour Guide

We paid to have the whole cart for ourselves, so we didn't have to wait for more people. And, it was worth it! Riding the cart through that huge complex, instead of walking, was the best decision we made.

The woman put on her tour guide hat, introducing and explaining everything very thoroughly. As we were riding down the main path, she explained the meaning behind those twelve pairs of colossal stone animal statues, what they represent, their characteristic and functionality....

A gentle breeze was ruffling our hair, blowing away the summer heat, as we glided through the park on the golf cart. Seann quietly listened to my translation without much expression, watching attentively and occasionally reaching his arm out to protect me from carelessly falling off the cart as our tour guide sped along the winding path.

Ming Tombs Statues

"Your husband is so nice to you!" The woman said.

"He..." I don't know how many times I had to explain to people and was really tired of clarifying our relationship, but this young woman was very sweet, and the complex is so big, we were going to spend a lot of time together, so I patiently told her, "He is not my husband, we are close friends."

"Oh... he is so handsome..... and rich, if you don't marry him, won't you worry that someone could steal him from you?"

"If some one could steal him from me, I would rather not marry him. Don't you think so?"

"I mean," she paused for a while, "He treats you so well, I don't think he would leave you, I think you should marry him!"

Many Chinese are kind and good-hearted, but tend to care too much about other people's business. I didn't want to continue discussing the topic.

Seann was unusually quiet. We had known each other for three years, spending nearly everyday together for about two and half of those years. Most of the time our conversations focus on spiritual and philosophical subjects, along with many other subjects that may not concern us directly, but we never discuss our relationship. We are not really girlfriend and boyfriend, but in some way we seem closer than that, and that's why many people have mistaken us for a married couple. So, what is our relationship? Sometimes I don't even know.

No matter the scenario or emotional state I was in, I couldn't deny the familiarity and closeness we feel about each other, which has nothing to do with our current lifetime. And in retrospect many of our disagreements were totally not making sense from our current situation, they seemed to be emotional baggage from the past.

One day, we were trying to figure out why we met.

"I don't think we meet again in this life is to continue a romance." Seann said, "If that's the case, we should be closer in age, and we would have met sooner."

"Then what do you think is the reason we met?"

"Maybe so that we learn something about each other that we weren't able to learn before. Or maybe to work out some unfinished business."

"I totally agree. Remember how you asked me, many times, why I always try to run away?"

"Yeah, did you figure out why?"

"Because in this life, I am free, so I can. Ha, ha!" I started laughing.

He laughed too, then continued. "But seriously, between us is a deeper connection, a deeper love."

Maybe so. Despite the seemingly irreconcilable differences in many areas, after all this time, we are still together.

I recalled the dream I had this morning. What kind of karmic bond keeps us together lifetime after lifetime?

Physicist and consciousness researcher Tom Campbell, author of *My Big TOE*[42], uses the analogy that life is like a video game. "We need to change from within, not just become a better actor or game player."

Every game comes with a predefined rule set. No matter how good a player we claim to be, we are restrained by the rules. We can't play our way out of the game world. In a way, the game designer is similar to the "architect" in the movie "The Matrix", he or she is the "God" of that game world. To get free from being confined by the rules written by others, we have to leap out of the game world, and become our own architect.

To reach that level of consciousness, Tom Campbell recommends that we "meditate". Meditation is a tool, just like the training wheels used when we were learning how to ride a bicycle. Once we learn, those training wheels were no longer needed. Of course, meditation is not the only tool, but it is easy to do and pretty effective. As long as we follow the basic principles, everybody can reach the same result no matter what religion we believe.

Basically, I agree with Tom. Meditation is an easy practice to help us obtain clarity and calmness, making it easier to differentiate what is mind chatter, and what is genuine intuition or inspiration. Meditation is also a way to help us let go of our ego's grip on our mind, and clear the accumulated dirt that's been covering the window to our inner self, so we can allow our soul to shine through.

But, what about karma? Is karma the reason we could become bound to a specific game? Is it possible to leap out of the game board without clearing karmic ties?

Jon Peniel in his book, *Children of the Law of One*[43] stated, "Karma is constantly being created, and life keeps trying to teach us something by providing us with our own self-created lessons - that explode in our faces."

How much do we have to suffer, before we realize that we need to change from within?

REFERENCES

37. [Photo]
Nanjing View (Nanjing, China)
intheeternal.com/en/id/827

38. [Location]
Ming Xiaoling, Nanjing
intheeternal.com/en/id/383

39. [Photo]
Nanjing Wall (Nanjing, China)
intheeternal.com/en/id/459

40. [Photo]

Ming Tombs Tour (Ming Tombs, Nanjing, China)

intheeternal.com/en/id/443

41. [Photo]

Ming Tombs Statues (Ming Tombs, Nanjing, China)

intheeternal.com/en/id/457

42. [Book]

Campbell, T. (2007) *My Big TOE*

intheeternal.com/en/id/777

43. [Book]

Peniel, J. (1997) *Children of the Law of One : Lost Teachings of Atlantis*

intheeternal.com/en/id/812

6

True Beauty

*"As we let our light shine, we
unconsciously give other people
permission, to do the same."*

— Nelson Mandela

I first visited Mainland China in 2001 with my colleague and friend
David. He invited me to join the consulting company he had
founded, and his friend, who was CEO of the Chinese subsidiary
of a European company, suggested he visit Beijing to explore some
opportunities.

David was on a junior Olympic swimming team in high school
and was still very fit, with blue eyes that reminded me of Paul
Newman. We met when I was teaching MCSE (Microsoft Certified
Systems Engineer) bootcamp at a network services company. He
was working out of the same office where my computer lab was
located, and he took couple of the classes I was teaching. We didn't
get close until my father got sick and past away. During that difficult period of my life, he was extra supportive so we spoke often
and became friends.

While we were in China, he mentioned that when he visited
Japan, he was frequently approached by girls who wanted to take
a picture with him. "Japanese girls are very aggressive, I was surprised!" he said. However, for the ten days we were in China
nothing like that happened, leaving him confused and surprised
again.

"Maybe Chinese girls are more conservative." I said, trying to mend his afflicted ego.

Fast forward eleven years, and not only girls, but boys and even older people were asking to take pictures with Seann. Why? Is it just because he is handsome? Or because the society is more open now?

When at the Forbidden City he was stopped several times for pictures, and again when touring "Qiao Family Courtyard", where a group of girls surrounded Seann, wanting to take picture with him. He sat down on a nearby bench looking tense, with hands on his knees, and eyes looking straight at the camera. The girls were giggling, switching seats, taking turns sitting next to him.....
I found it entertaining and took a couple of pictures myself.

Qiao Courtyard Photo Op   Shaolin Photo Op

Through out the whole charade, Seann was motionless with a poker face, and did not pay any attention to the girls. After they finished the photo op, Seann got up, tapped me on my shoulder and turned to walk quickly in the opposite direction of the tourists. Finally he found a remote corner in a quiet garden and stopped. I was just barely catching up with his fast pace and was still out of breath.

"Can you explain why we are here?" He asked exasperatedly.

"This is a famous tourist spot."

"Why do so many people want to take pictures with me?"

"Because you are a good looking American, and you have blue eyes."

Then he became really irritated. "To value a person based only on their look is the most ridiculous and shallow behavior."

"Well, strangers don't know you, all they can see is how you look. If you don't like it, you can refuse to take pictures with them, why blame me for it?"

"That's not what I mean," he noticed that I wasn't happy with his attitude, "it's fine, they are innocent. And I wasn't blaming you either."

"Maybe I was wrong, people were not attracted by your look but your inner light."

"Yeah, right." he said, laughing.

"Ha! Now you can't complain any more." I said to myself with a secret smile. Although, I do agree with his viewpoint. True beauty lies within.

Founder of the famous brand Chanel, Coco Chanel said, "There are no ugly women in the world, just lazy ones." (Chanel video *Reincarnation*)[47]

With high tech cosmetics and plastic surgery widely available today, that quote seems more true than ever. However, I happen to be the lazy one. I don't like to cover my face with cosmetics, and really don't like to wear jewelry.

After graduating from UCSB Graduate school, I learned to put on makeup for job interviews. On the second day of my first job, I went to the office with no makeup on and hardly any of my colleagues noticed. So I happily stayed away from the cosmetics for most of my life.

While working as an MCT (Microsoft Certified Trainer) in my early 40's, I usually wore lipstick on the first day of training, and then nothing after that. My students, both male and female, would often hang around after class. One day the secretary, who was young and pretty and wore full makeup everyday, commented on how unusual it was for students to be so engaged with the instructor.

However, one of my students who could see the subtle energy field, or "aura" as some spiritual traditions call it, and he understood why people liked being around me. Laurel, who was one of the original engineers with the company, had been very anti-certification. Before he arrived at the class, some of my old students warned me about him, even my boss called from Boston to tell me be extra careful.

In order to receive the MCSE certificate, people need to pass six exams. A lot of the Americans seemed not so good at taking tests. Being a computer engineer, I noticed that the subjects are not difficult, but the tests are tricky. I, on the other hand, grew up in Taiwan, and while I may not be the best engineer, I am really good at passing exams. As a result, in addition to teaching the subject matter, I also taught my students how to pass the exams. If they failed to pass, I would give them individual tutoring sessions and encourage them to try again. Therefore, my students had very high passing rate compared to other MCSE instructors.

Friday night after the first week ended, I took the class out to dinner as usual. Laurel requested to go to The Wizard Restaurant next to Universal Studios. The air conditioning was too strong, so I crossed my arms and was contemplating if I should go down to the gift shop to buy a blanket. Laurel asked me to extend my arm out, then he started tapping my wrist. A few moments later I warmed up.

"Those are all fake," he pointed to the magicians on stage, then pointed to my wrist, "this is real."

"You know Qigong?" I asked him.

"No, I'm not that patient, this is only simple tapping"[48] He turned to eat his dinner and said casually, "you look nice today."

At the end of the three weeks bootcamp, Laurel came to my office to say goodbye. "Thank you. I don't know what magic you used to help me pass all those exams."

I smiled and noticed that Laurel was looking at the space above my shoulder and on top of my head with soft, unfocused eyesight, "Have you read *Celestine Prophecy*?" He asked.

"Of course!"

"You practice Qigong so you should understand Qi. Energy, vibration, the aura, whatever you want to call it, it's real."

"Oh, you were looking at my aura?"

"Compared with three weeks ago, your aura is much dimer now. Don't devote so much energy to your students, or your children. You should take better care of yourself first. Dress up more, like the other night at dinner. You have to know, at the current stage of human evolution, not many people can actually see the aura. In other words, hardly anyone can see your inner beauty, and even though they may feel it, they don't know what it is."

"Don't worry, I will have a good rest after you guys leave. I typically get a two-week break between classes."

"Remember to practice what I taught you, and continue practicing Qigong. That is the real magic you possess!"

One of the things Laurel taught me was how to see the aura. I practiced enough that I could see it, so I know it's real. But I purposely do not try to see the aura around people. I feel that is almost an invasion of people's privacy. Truthfully, I don't want to know other people's business, life is complicated enough as it is.

The following Monday afternoon, I went to the office after a walk on the beach. A huge bouquet of roses sat right in the center of my desk. I opened the card, it said, "I hope these flowers can remind you how beautiful you really are! But in order to get people's appreciation, a beautiful thing still requires time and effort to maintain it's beauty."

There was no signature.

Of course I didn't take Laurel's advice, and continued being a lazy woman. My life partner, assuming I met him someday, would see who I really am, I thought egoistically.

And when that person did finally show up, I was irritated by him very often, and for many years.

Los Angeles County, California
June 2010

"Good Diamond! Are there anymore? Go get some more!"

Smart Dogs

One day I came home after work and went to look for Seann, who was in the backyard watching the dogs chewing my shoes. Apparently Diamond, my Siberian Husky, opened the side door to the garage and dug my leather shoes out, then started chewing on them.

When Diamond saw me she knew she did something bad, so she ran quickly to the rocky hillside to hide. Dean, my Golden Retriever, as usual had no clue what he had done, and was happily wagging his tail welcoming me home. I picked up my beautiful Italian shoes, now chewed beyond recognition, and was just about to yell at Seann, when he attempted to interject with his typical light hearted humor, "High heel shoes are one of the most useless inventions. You should thank Diamond for helping you get rid of them. And by the way, I just got here, they did this on their own. Smart dogs!"

The more we felt comfortable with each other, the more comments he had regarding my appearance.

"The suit you are wearing looks tight, are you comfortable?"

"The color of your lipstick doesn't match your skin, do you have to put lipstick on? The natural look is always the best!"

"I can see through your skirt under the sun, is it necessary to wear that skirt?"

"Those shoes look uncomfortable....."

When I would show my frustration with his comments, he would say something like, "I'm only trying to help! Wearing something comfortable is the most important thing. No need to follow fashion, or care how other people look at you."

"It's easy for you to say, how about you?" I asked him when he first told me to stop trying to impress people.

"For many years I always wore my uniform, a black t-shirt and khaki shorts, they were cleanly pressed and comfortable and I had a closet full of them. I would even wear them when first meeting my clients, because it was hot in Texas, and they typically dress casually at home too. Besides, what they care about is my ability to do my job, not what I wear."

I could never win argument against him, and was often reminded of what Laurel said, "Be careful what you wish for, it might come true!"

When we lived in northern California, especially while living in the mountains, Seann was always concerned when I went grocery shopping, and would go with me whenever he could. While in the supermarket checkout line, I would often flip through the magazines on display.

One day he caught me looking at Vanity Fair. "Those women all have ugly energy! I don't understand why you would be interested."

"So, in your eyes there are no pretty woman?"

"I didn't say that...she is pretty." I happened to have flipped to a page with Jennifer Lawrence on it. She had short blond hair with light make up and casual clothes, and was smiling naturally.

"Actually, why don't you look at yourself?" He said. "You are honest, ethical, and you truly care about other people. That kind of inner beauty will never grow old."

Whoa, I thought, what's wrong with him today?

"And, you are knowledgeable, humble, intelligent, and always open to learn new things."

I was going to make some jokes but noticed his serious stance so I kept quiet.

He's right, people might appreciate or prefer different kinds of beauty. Most people care probably a little too much how other people view them, but overlook their own inner virtues.

If we would appreciate and be grateful for what we already have within us, recognizing our own value and making peace with our inner self, we can bring harmony into our environment. If we practice understanding, kindness, and appreciation, we might be able to remain peaceful even during the most difficult circumstances.

Then, maybe, we can help create a more peaceful world.

REFERENCES

44. [Photo]

True Beauty (Hsi Lai Temple, California)

intheeternal.com/en/id/819

45. [Photo]

Qiao Photo (Qiao Courtyard, Shanxi, China)

intheeternal.com/en/id/460

46. [Photo]

Shaolin Photo (Shaolin Temple, China)

intheeternal.com/en/id/548

47. [Note]

Chanel - Reincarnation Video

intheeternal.com/en/id/526

48. [Link]

Tapping : tapping.com website

intheeternal.com/en/id/778

49. [Photo]

Smart Dogs (Los Angeles County)

intheeternal.com/en/id/432

7

Abundance

"... unless each soul entity (and this entity
especially) makes the world better,
that corner or place of
the world a little better,
a little bit more hopeful,
a little bit more patient,
showing a little more of brotherly love,
a little more of kindness,
a little more of long suffering
- by the very words and deeds of the entity,
the life is a failure..."

— Edgar Cayce

Beijing, China
July 2012

In the States we rarely use cash, and based on my previous visits to China, I knew credit cards are not as widely accepted as in most western countries. So, I exchanged some US dollars to RMB when we arrived. Seann, who is normally generous, turned into Santa Claus.

"Money is like air or water, it needs circulation." He said smiling. "Have I told you the story about what happened when I gave that disabled veteran $100?"

"Yes, 100 times!" I rolled my eyes.

"Then you must have forgotten, so I'll just tell you the 101st time." He said, ignoring my protest. "Even though I rarely gave money to panhandlers, I decided to give the guy money because if he was outside in the rain on Christmas weekend he probably needed it. All I had was a $100 bill, so I gave it to him, wished him Merry Christmas, and left."

"And your client gave you a Christmas card with $100 in it when you were leaving the job site."

"Yeah, within an hour I got that $100 back. Exactly."

"Well, if you didn't give him the $100, you would have $200 in your wallet." I hadn't pointed that out the previous times he mentioned that story, but today I didn't hesitate, even knowing he might object.

"I only carried the $100 for an emergency," he ignored my provoking comment, "but that $100 could help him have a nicer Christmas, so why not? Besides, it's possible the client only decided to give me the $100 because she felt my happy and generous mood."

Earlier in the day we had visited the Temple of Heaven. We wanted to see it before leaving Beijing, but when it was time to leave the Temple, traffic was really, really bad. I was worried that we might miss the train so instead of sitting in traffic in a taxi, we hired a tricycle. We agreed to pay 50 RMB and asked him to get us back to the hotel quickly, which seemed fair as the taxi from the hotel to the Temple that morning had only cost 10 RMB.

The driver understood we were in a hurry, and did put in extra effort, going down small side streets while skillfully dodging pedestrians and people on motorbikes. When we arrived at the hotel a short time later, I gave him 70 RMB, feeling generous. He took it, then looked at Seann and said, "One person 50, two people 100."

Temple Of Heaven

I was stunned. The Hotel security officer walked over and asked if there were any problem. I didn't want to get the tricycle driver in trouble, so I said, "Everything is fine." Then turned to ask Seann if he had any change. Seann pulled out a 100 RMB bill and the driver took it, putting all 170 RMB in his pocket, thanking Seann. Seann said "謝謝" (thank you in Chinese) to him too.

At the train station, after replaying the exchange with the driver over and over, getting more frustrated each time, I couldn't hold my frustration and exploded on him. "You are always like that!"

"Like what?" He looked at me, confused. "What are you talking about?"

"You let people take advantage of us." I said, in a frustrated tone.

It took a few seconds, then he realized I was upset with how he handled the tricycle driver. "He put in a lot of extra effort to get us back to hotel in time, pedaling as hard as he could and weaving thru the side streets, otherwise we might have missed the train."

"I know, but..."

He turned away, looking around the station, lost in thought. Then he looked at me like he remembered something, "Money is not ours, it's only in our possession for us to make use of it." He paused for a few seconds, then continued. "There is a story in the Bible that talks about utilizing what you have been given."

I could tell Seann had gotten into his preacher mode. When in that mode he would tell story after story, many times with good insights. We were going to be at the station for a while, so it was a good time for a long conversation.

"As I recall, the story is essentially that a master gave money to a handful of servants, and a few years later asked what they did with it. He congratulated the servants who did something with it, but was angry at the servant who buried the money, afraid he might loose it. The general idea is that we are given things so that we can make use of them. Some people are given talents or abilities, and others wisdom or insights. Often the things we are good at and enjoy doing, like art, dance, music, or making things, are gifts we have been given to share. In my case, it might be helping you to see things differently..."

He looked at me with a smile on his face, saw that I wasn't smiling in return, then continued attentively...

"But seriously, we are given things so that we can share them. What good would come from the wisdom of Lao-Tzu, or Siddhartha, if they sat alone in the forest and didn't share what they knew?"

I was quiet and still in a negative mood, but showed my interest in his story...

"A lot of the people I did work for, not all, but a lot of them, were very generous, taking care of the people who worked for them. Sometimes, they would agree to have the landscaper do something they might not need, so the landscaper and his crew could have something to do. Or in my case, they might not question proposals or invoices that I presented, paying immediately after the work was finished. It was the little things that I noticed, but it's the little things that matter."

He looked over my shoulder for a few seconds, then looked at me and smiled, as if he knew I might object to what he was about to say. "In my view, it's not because they were wealthy that they were generous, their generous nature is the reason they became wealthy. The attitude that there is enough for everyone, creates that outcome for them too."

"I do that for the people who worked on my houses too, but it doesn't always work like that, it's not that simple."

He was quiet for a moment, then smiled and asked, "Are you sure?"

"I don't know." I said, but I knew he was probably right. Maybe that's why the construction process for my house went smoothly.

"You are right though. Things may not be that simple." He said, extending his arms out to protect me from being pushed by other people, and continuing with his reasoning. "A lot of people aren't wealthy, and can't necessarily be very generous, because they don't have much themselves. And even if they are generous with their time, helping people in different ways, it may not come back to them immediately, or in ways they could notice."

"Yes, exactly!" I interjected, "That's what I meant."

"I was speaking from the perspective of middle class westerner," he said, agreeing with my reply, "not necessarily a fisherman in Central America, or a factory worker in Vietnam." He looked around the crowd, as if to get a sense of how some of the people around us might react to what he was saying.

"However, it's still true, just on a different scale. In some cases it may take longer for the energy associated with good deeds to accumulate, and for their positive effects to show up in noticeable ways, but they do show up. The little things make a difference, they do matter. And the more we consciously practice being generous, the more we will notice the effects."

Nevada County, California
April 2012

For many years we would start each day with what we called "Coffee Talk". Usually it was about random topics or current events, but sometimes Seann would get into his philosopher mode.

"The crystals are bright this morning. Even before I opened the window, the clear quartz was shining." I said one morning while making coffee.

"What is this one again?" Seann asked, pointing to a Citrine crystal ball I bought many years earlier.

"It's some sort of crystal that suppose could amplify energy." I said, feeling bad for spending so much for it. "I was terrible, I spent so much money..."

"It doesn't matter, it brought you here. It's all just experience, no regrets." He said, trying to cheer me up.

"It's in your nature to buy crystals, either because they make you feel good, or to help the people selling them. It's in your nature to want to help people. It's in your nature to do things that are fun. It's just the way you are, and there isn't anything wrong with that."

Seann held the crystal ball up to the beams of sunlight coming into the window. "Don't beat yourself up about spending money on this crystal, it's a beautiful thing."

I handed him the coffee.

"I did the same thing. But, I also have a lot of good memories. What I remember is taking lots of long road trips and hiking in State and National Parks, not how much I spent on hotels or fuel. I also went on a lot of scuba diving trips, flew a plane, jumped out of a plane, and was taken for a ride in a customer's Carrera GT[52]. Those are the things that I remember, not how much money I spent on scuba gear, or how much more money I could have made if I had charged the customer with the exotic car collection for every hour I spent working on his home automation system.

So don't make everything about how much something costs. That has little relevance to the way life really works, and it has even less relevance in the spiritual realms. When you die, you are not going to give any thought to how much money you spent. What you are going to remember are the kinds of experiences you had, and what you were brave enough to do in your life.

That is why I went to North Carolina. I walked away from a lot of opportunities, things I could have made a lot of money doing, because more than anything else, I wanted to be independent. Money and status were never the main motivation for me, freedom was more important. And, because I wasn't chasing after money, we met.

So, I would say if you have spent money buying beautiful things like this crystal, congratulations! We need more art and craftsmanship in the world, and directing your energy towards things of beauty, like this crystal, helps."

Beijing, China
July 2012

It was a relatively short train ride, so we rode in the regular sitting cabin. It was really difficult for me to sit there drinking tea, while watching people who were not able to get seats, standing or sitting in the walk way, especially if they were old or with children. I would give up my seat, and Seann's too, but among all those people who should I give the seats to? Suddenly, I felt very tired so I closed my eyes to reflect on our conversation at the station.

We all have different world views that have shaped us. "Real wealth is not the accumulation of things", had been one of my father's core beliefs. Seann's empathetic generosity fits my attitude toward life, and that has been one of the reasons that we get along so well.

— 今 —

I remembered one incident at a gas station in Santa Rosa, shortly after we moved from Los Angeles to northern California. I had gone inside to use the restroom, and when I came out I saw a young man with a toddler siting on his shoulder talking with Seann at the pump. Seann pulled out a bill from his wallet and gave it to the man.

We had bought something earlier, so I knew he had two bills in his wallet, one $10 and one $20. I was thinking, "He is just like my dad, even if he only has one dollar in his pocket, he would find a way to give it out."

While driving away from the gas station, Seann was still looking at the rear view mirror, and seemed sad.

"You gave him $20 huh!" I said, trying to show that I knew what happened.

"No, I gave him $10.... I should have given him the $20." He said, obviously regretting it. "It must be tough to be stranded on the road with a child."

I was silent, knowing the reason he didn't give out the $20 was probably because he didn't want to upset me.

"You know, there are many situations in life where we regret what we did or didn't do, when it was too late to take any action. This is different." I said. "You can change it easily."

He looked at me, with sparkles in his eyes, turned the car around, and smiled.

We found that stranded couple in the supermarket parking lot at the back of the gas station, standing by an older model car. Even though they were stranded, the young parents seemed in good spirits, playing with their son and laughing.

"I'll be right back." Seann said, tapping my hand.

Sitting in the car, watching him walking toward them, my eyes started to tear. That moment, I felt so wealthy and content. I had to agree with him, money is only a tool, not the purpose of life. The real abundance is what we are gifted or entrusted with from the infinite Universe, so we can help others by sharing it.

— 今 —

But, that was then, this is now. I opened my eyes and looked at Seann, trying to stay calm. Even though I knew all of that, I still worried sometimes.

"With the way you are spending money these last few days," I said in a worried tone, "the money we budgeted for two months in China probably will barely last one month."

"Then, it might mean we only need to stay in China for one month." He said in his typical optimistic demeanor, looking out the window as the scenery was quickly passing by.

In the end, we didn't even stay for a month. We left Nanjing for Taipei after 19 days, and the reason had nothing to do with money.

REFERENCES

50. [Photo]
    Lithia Park (Ashland, Oregon)
    intheeternal.com/en/id/824

51. [Photo]
    Temple of Heaven (Beijing, China)
    intheeternal.com/en/id/467

52. [Link]
    Carrera GT : DuPont Registry website
    intheeternal.com/en/id/779

8

Waking Dream

"Of this I am sure, that we are here
for a purpose. And we go on.
Mind and memory, they are eternal."

— Henry Ford

Ming Tombs, Nanjing, China
July 2012

"Do you remember Ahtun Re saying that the original architecture
of Ming Xiaoling is similar to the Forbidden City, because both were
based on Zhu Gong's design?" I asked Seann. He looked at me and
nodded, then turned back to the information displays on the wall,
waiting for me to finish my thoughts.

I turned to look at the large picture display, trying to put my
thoughts into words, and suddenly felt like I was being pulled into
a trance...the exhibition hall in front of me transformed into the
dreamscape of the dream from earlier that morning. Seann seemed
fading into it also, transforming into an ancient person.

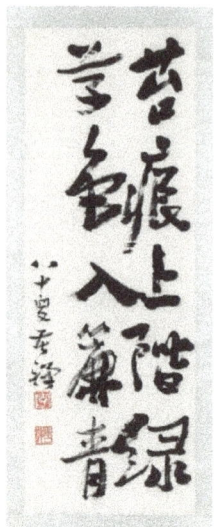

My Humble Abode

I followed Seann into a garden manor. A
butler came up to him and said, "your
hi..." stopping abruptly after seeing me.

"My brother Chen's horse is outside, bring
it to the stable," Seann instructed the butler
in a firm voice, "take good care of him."

The manor was immense, with simple but
elegant furnishings. I followed him into a
courtyard surrounded by bamboo. On
top of the opening doorway, there was
a plaque with two words, Meditation Hall.

Inside the courtyard was a grassy area with a few trees
along the walls. We walked through the courtyard
and came to what looked like a study. As I stepped
into the room, I saw a writing hanging on the wall,

Emerald moss creeping up
turned stone stairs green,
Reflection of grass colored curtains
with blueish hue.

"Ah! Liu Yuxi's "The Inscriptions of
My Humble Abode... Which powerful
man of the court did you provoke?"

He looked back at me with astonishment and
admiration, then said indifferently, "the emperor."

Ming Xiaoling

I was jolted and woke up to reality instantaneously, but Seann was no where in sight. I went outside, and saw him speaking angrily at two young boys. It's strange, I've never seen him be mean to anyone. The boys couldn't understand his English, but they seemed to know what he was talking about, so they turned and ran away.

"What's going on?"

"Those inconsiderate children!" He squatted down and looked at the corners of the wall...... Oh! Slugs. I've never seen such big slugs, about ten centimeters long in light grayish brown color.

"What's wrong?"

"Those kids grabbed them off the ground and threw them at the stone wall." He pushed one of them onto a big leaf with a branch, "Do you think this one will survive?"

"I don't know."

He pushed the slugs one by one onto the leaves and put them into the bushes while whispering, "Go farther away, don't come to the road."

— 今 —

Later that night at the hotel, while reading the book I bought at Shaolin Temple, I looked over at Seann. He was on his laptop as usual, and was looking irritated again.

"I'm fine, don't assume something is wrong." The irritated guy noticed I was staring at him and seemed to have read my mind. I smiled at him and continued reading my book. Suddenly, a paragraph in the book caught my attention...

> Renshan Yi Gong (1340-1405) became a monk at the Changshou Monastery in Dengzhou. After he came out of his Buddhism training, he presided over great temples in Pingyang, Taiyuan, Jiexiu, and Jiaocheng in Shanxi province. He exemplified on Vipassana (Ritsu) and was a highly respected bhikkhu master. In the 16th year of Hongwu (1383), by order of the King of Jin, he was the Abbot of Chongshan Temple in Taiyuan for ten years. In the 26th year of Hongwu (1393), by order of the King of Zhou, he became the Abbot at Shaolin Temple for 13 years (1393-1405). In May of 1405, he was summoned to Beijing for heading a celebration puja and passed away on September 22 that year.

"Whoa, wow! So that's what happened. That makes things much more clear." I said to myself.

"What?" Seann asked.

I explained what the book said, and what it meant.

Essentially, the King of Jin, who was Emperor HongWu's 3rd son Zhu Gong[56], asked Renshen Yi Gong to be the Abbot of a Temple dedicated to his mother. Then later, Yi Gong became Abbot of Shaolin. The relationship between Zhu Gong and Renshen Yi Gong played a big role in what happened after Hong Wu died, and his 4th son Zhu Di usurped the throne.

"So, Zhu Gong asked him to be the Abbot at the Temple dedicated to his mother, Empress Ma?"

"Yeah, Chongshan Temple. Then he became head of Shaolin Temple."

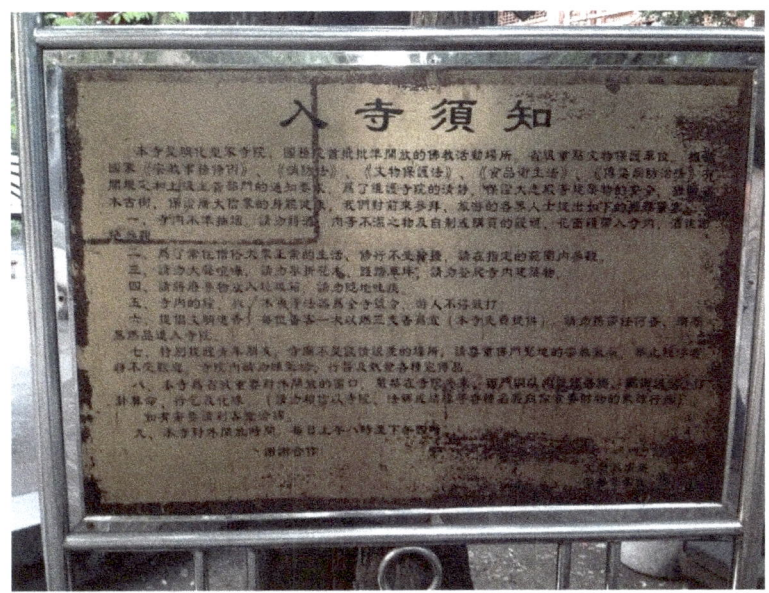

Chongshan History

"So they probably knew each other pretty well. Which means, if Zhu Gong wanted to stay out of the conflict after his brothers died, Shaolin would be a safe place to be. That also means what Ahtun Re and the old monk from Shaolin Temple said is true."

"I guess so!"

Where do I begin?

Shirley MacLaine, the Oscar award winning actress, made a very avant-garde mini-series in 1987, based on her autobiographical book, *Out On a Limb*[58]. In the movie, Shirley plays herself, traveling around the world in pursuit of answers to her spiritual quest. Kevin Ryerson[13], who also plays himself in the movie, is an intuitive and trance channel, similar to Edgar Cayce.

Ahtun Re[59] is one of the spirit guides that Kevin has a working relationship with. He was an Egyptian priest during the Akhenaten era, more than 3,000 years ago. Ahtun was of Nubian descent and was the leader of the Egyptian army. After loosing his family in a battle, he renounced violence and became a priest. When he transitioned in that lifetime more than 3,000 years ago, he decided not to reincarnate again in order to stay in the higher spiritual realms to help guide those in need. Because of his training in the priesthood, he is able to access what we call the Akashic Records, also known as "The Book of Life".

During his research into reincarnation, Seann found Dr.Walter Semkiw's book *Return of the Revolutionaries*[60], which led to Kevin Ryerson. In the mid-1990s, my Qigong teacher, Jennifer Sun, rented an apartment from Shirley on the Malibu beachfront. Shirley also studied Wuji Qigong with her, and the scene which Kevin appeared in *Out On A Limb* was shot at Shirley's apartment, above the one Jennifer was renting.

Based on all of that synchronicity, and his work with Walter Semkiw, we felt that Kevin could help us to verify and understand what we believed to be true about our own past life connection.

Los Angeles County, California
March 2010

The first time we spoke with Kevin, we felt very comfortable with him. Although he has a very unique ability, and appeared in Shirley's movie, he is very humble and easy-going. Our first session with Kevin was shortly after we returned from a spiritual workshop in Guatemala.

Lake Atitlan

While we hoped the workshop would help clarify our past life connection, it made things more confusing than before. We left the workshop early and spent the rest of our time in Guatemala exploring Panajachel, a culture rich lakeside city. After we returned to California, I actually started questioning why we should care so much about past lives, and wondered if we should just let it go.

When the day came for Seann's first session with Kevin, I was going to leave the room, but he asked me to stay. Knowing that Seann wanted to know about reincarnation and past lives, Kevin's consciousness receded to let spirit speak thru him, and Ahtun Re was the guide who showed up.

"Ah! I am a being called Ahtun Re and I have come to speak with you..."

Seann hesitated, "I have a few questions about a possible past lifetime."

"Can you describe elements of this past life please?" Ahtun Re asked.

Seann looked at me, "uh... wanting some clarification on that. Assuming this is true, it was about 100 years ago, in China."

"Oh that's a drop in the bucket when you are 3,000 years old." Ahtun Re joked. "What's a couple of centuries among friends? Please continue..."

"Yes. So, I've met someone who apparently, assuming this is true, that I knew back then..."

"I understand." he said. "Do you feel you know who you were?"

"Yes."

"Describe please." he asked.

"Uh, I was a...um..."

"Don't be shy, after 3000 years you have seen just about every-thing." Ahtun Re said jokingly.

"Understand, yes. Uh, it seems based on some of my life expe-rience, some pictures and some other things, that I was a, um...an emperor." Seann said in a very hesitant tone.

"That's interesting. I am not sure that is so unusual. What do know of this emperor?"

Seann hesitated, his expression suddenly overcome with sad-ness. "I know that he lived quite a tragic life. There was a lot of...I know quite a bit about his experience."

"Describe please, what you have affinity with."

"Many of the things that happened in his experience, some of the tragedies that happened in his experience, the effects of that, uh, have affected me in my life. Meaning, some things that I have been concerned about, fearful of, actually relate perfectly with that life experience."

"In other words you share the same vibration, anxieties, the same personality type?"

"That is correct."

"Do you have the approximate birthdate of the fellow?" Ahtun Re asked.

"August 14th, 1871."

"One moment... This emperor was caught up in the affairs of the transition of his country in it's modernization, the east and west playing what became known as the opium wars and about the time period of the Boxer Rebellion. In other words, he was involved in the modernization of his country, and he was caught in between various political entities. One moment... are you looking for the meaning of this life?"

"I am looking for, uh... yes, confirmation, clarification, meaning, yes." Seann said, more directly.

"I understand. Well, may I explain?"

"Please."

"One moment... This emperor when he lived, in some of his poetry it was known that he also wished he had been a common man. That he had not been born into the emperor-ship at all. He was a person caught between two ages and wished to preserve the beauty of the culture, but also harnessing the benefits of the modern emerging world to the benefit of his nation. In many ways he was also a gifted poet, and to a certain degree an artist, and he wasn't a weak leader, but he was caught between powerful industrial forces. His country had been stripped of many of it's resources thru so called colonialism, and corruption in the court. Do you follow?"

Seann had been looking out the window, listening intently. "Oh yes." he said.

"In many ways, he wished to try and preserve the spiritual dimensions of his culture, which he did not consider to be superstition, but legitimate elements of his Chinese and Asian culture. And, at the same time again, to merge with the benefits of the still emerging modern industrial period. And, not to see his nation exploited, carved up, into it's various components. Do you understand?"

"Yes."

"May I now explain to you why you are incarnate in this period?"

"Please."

"Notice that the historical figure left the body at the turn of the century, when there was truly a crystallization of the emergence of the confluences that make up the modern identity. The emergence of the automobile, the plane, but it is only now in your 21st century, that your consciousness of that lifetime is beginning to emerge, almost around the date that the historical figure left the body. The reason for that is several fold, may I describe please?"

"Please."

"China was considered to be the birthplace of many key advancements, and is considered much like India to be one of the mother cultures. In fact at one time if it hadn't closed it's borders, it could have actually, with it's great trade seat, many centuries earlier, it could have taken a position in world leadership. Do you follow?"

"Yes."

"Nowadays, it is interesting that you have settled into the so-called computer arts, and what is interesting is this internet tool. One of the innovations that China brought about, which was most revolutionary, was movable type, and paper. As these things worked there way to Europe, thru that Marco Polo fellow, it caused the very roots of the Industrial Revolution that eventually over-whelmed the Asian and the Chinese identity. Now, within the mother culture called China, or Qin, there is the struggle with the emerging internet culture which is like the new printed word, it is like the new digital paper. That is intriguing isn't it?"

"Yes."

"I do believe there is a part of you that wishes to tap into an element of the human spirit, and wishes to bring that knowledge of spirit to a broader range of people, thru your so called author-ship. One of the things that this emperor originally wished was to preserve the spiritual core, what he felt was the true treasures of China such as the Tao, or Confucianism, or the preferred spiritual philosophy which he knew the west would not provide. Do you follow?"

"Yes." Seann said, looking at me as if he was overwhelmed.

I also felt the need for a break, so I slowly made my way to the door, leaving Seann alone with Ahtun Re. My dogs saw me step out onto the balcony, quickly running up the spiral stairs to say hello. The landscaper waved as he was pulling up the driveway to do his weekly yard maintenance.

As I sat outside enjoying the cool breeze and cloudless southern California sky, I thought about how much my life had changed since meeting Seann. So much had happened, but it had only been about 8 months. After I regained my composure, I decided to go back inside, knowing that the session would probably be ending soon.

"May I describe to you one or two other quick lives?" Ahtun Re asked.

Seann had a look of surprise on his face, "Please."

"One moment. You had been there at the founding of China, of Qin. And...there was... one moment... there was the shifting of the capital to the contemporary city of Peking. The emperor who built the so-called Forbidden City, was considered to be a Usurper, do you understand?"

"Yes." Seann looked at me, remembering that my QiGong teacher said I had a lifetime in the early Ming Dynasty.

"The true emperor lived in a city of great beauty, poetry and scholarship, the original capital. In that lifetime, you had been a member of the royal family, and could have even been in line for the throne. But you preferred the life of a scholar, and wanted to stay as far away from family politics as you possibly could. Isn't that interesting?"

"Yes, it is." Seann said, smiling.

"Now, in that lifetime you got to pursue depth of knowledge, depth of scholarship. And, you felt that the capital city should be a model for other cities built around China. In other words, a system or a network of sort of, scholar-priests. You had even gone so far as to map out the so-called Feng Shui of the cities, where they would be placed. You had mapped China's complex rivers and canal systems... Do you follow?"

"Yes."

"But, when the Usurper came along, he actually came across some of your plans, and saw some of the canal systems you had designed. And, it became a model for the so-called Forbidden City, but he turned it into a military court. He turned the canal systems into a means of transporting the materials to build his egotistical city, which essentially was on a rather vast...wasteland. Isn't that interesting?"

"Yes."

"In that lifetime, when your older brothers were murdered, you withdrew into some of the temple complexes in the Shaolin area. And, you never stepped forward to exercise what could have been your right to claim the throne. One moment... You felt that perhaps some of the nations suffering could have come from that. Simply put, I suppose in that last lifetime, you may have seen the industrial powers of the world carving up China, so perhaps you took on that identity or that incarnation, out of a sense of karmic accountability. Do you follow?"

We looked at each other, astonished. What Ahtun Re said made perfect sense, but was completely unexpected.

In follow-up sessions with Ahtun Re we were able to confirm that Guangxu's fate was related to a lifetime he had in the Ming Dynasty as Zhu Gong[56], which we discuss in Chapter 20. And, the lifetime as Zhu Gong was related to an even earlier lifetime as Fusu[62], eldest son of the First Emperor of China, builder of the Terracotta Army. We were also able to confirm I was there during all of those lifetimes, which made our story much more complicated than we realized.

As the session was coming to an end, Ahtun Re mentioned a few other lifetimes.

"Many of your incarnations have been with settled peoples, such as the Mayans. And, you had been there during the building of the city known as Angkor Wat[63]. You were incarnate during the time period of Akhenaten[64], who was the predecessor of Tutankhamun, when he built his city of Akhetaten. You were usually involved when societies were beginning to reinvent themselves. You have come to know that those social orders will not survive if they are only secular, they must have a soul or a spiritual dimension..."

It took many years to understand what Ahtun Re was trying to communicate. However, it is now clear that Zhu Gong reincarnated as the Guangxu Emperor, out of a sense of karmic accountability. And, Seann learned about those lifetimes, so that he can help illustrate some of the principles of reincarnation.

The stories told in this book are just the beginning, Book 2 will cover some of the other lifetimes Ahtun Re has mentioned, in more detail.

REFERENCES

53. [Photo]
     Ming Xiaoling (Nanjing, China)
     intheeternal.com/en/id/458

54. [Image]
     My Humble Abode
     intheeternal.com/en/id/444

55. [Photo]
     Ming Tombs Walkway (Ming Tombs, Nanjing, China)
     intheeternal.com/en/id/539

56. [Note]
Zhu Gong : Son of Hongwu Emperor
intheeternal.com/en/id/521

57. [Photo]
Chongshan History (Chongshan Temple, Shanxi, China)
intheeternal.com/en/id/452

58. [Book]
MacLaine, S. (1983) *Out on a Limb*
intheeternal.com/en/id/815

13. [Note]
Kevin Ryerson : About
intheeternal.com/en/id/589

59. [Note]
Ahtun Re : About
intheeternal.com/en/id/637

60. [Book]
Semkiw, W. (2002) *Return of the Revolutionaries*
intheeternal.com/en/id/814

61. [Photo]
Lake Atitlan (Lake Atitlan, Guatemala)
intheeternal.com/en/id/471

62. [Note]

Fusu : Son of the First Emperor

intheeternal.com/en/id/522

63. [Location]

Angkor Wat

intheeternal.com/en/id/532

64. [Link]

Akhenaten : Egyptian Pharaoh

intheeternal.com/en/id/634

9

Shaolin Myth

"Future never comes as future, it unfolds as the present moment."

— Eckhart Tolle

Shaolin Temple is completely different than I expected. The Buddhist temple has become a Disneyland full of commercialized illusions. If you'd like to try your luck and see if you could meet a martial arts master and learn a few amazing moves, or listen to some life-changing inspirational enlightenment talks, you might be disappointed. Is it possible to have any mystical experience in this crowded Da Guan Yuan[66]?

On the roadside, in a sparse forest, there is a small, inconspicuous temple. Seann insisted on going there to take a look. A stone tablet in front of the temple reads, "Shaolin Temple Ancestral Hall", a place of worship for the ancestors of the Shaolin monks.

The door of the shrine was closed and there were only a few people around. "It's nice to have some peace and quiet." I thought. Just before we sat down on the side of the shrine, the door opened and an old monk peeked out, but when he saw Seann, he was surprised and closed the door promptly.

"Let's go," I said, "we should not disturb him."

As I was talking, the door opened again. This time it opened wide and the old monk came out to anchor the door at it's place.

"He opened the door again," Seann nudged me, "you go over and ask."

Shaolin Ancestral Hall

"Ask what?"

"He's looking at you."

I turned my head saw the old monk smile and waved at me. I had to walk over to give him a salute, "Hello Master!"

"Come in, come in!" He reached out and pointed into the shrine, then turned back and waved at Seann, inviting him to come in too.

When I stepped through the threshold, the monk put a string of huge Buddhist beads around my neck, gestured for me to kneel in front of the altar, and said to me, "Follow me."

"What about him?" I pointed to Seann.

"He doesn't have to, just let him stay on the side."

I breathed a sigh of relief. Seann had always liked to visit Buddhist temples, but never bowed to pay respect. He insisted that the true respect is in the heart, not any kind of formality.

When the ceremony was done, I got up and took several hundred RMB bills from my purse and handed it to the monk, saying apologetically, "I'm sorry I didn't bring any red envelopes on the trip." He pushed the money back to me, refusing to accept it, and gestured for me to sit down.

I tried to take the beads off, but he shook his hand and said, "keep them on." Then he gave me some advice on how to get along with Seann as a couple, including in some very private situations.

"We're just friends, not a couple." I said awkwardly.

He smiled and looked at Seann, ignored my explanation, and continued to give me advice. I thought to myself, Seann and I have known each other for three years, and we've been together for most of the last two and a half years, and I don't even know all his preferences. How could this monk know?

When he finished talking, he looked at Seann and asked, "Does he have any questions for me?"

Seann nudged me, "Did you ask?" I stared back at him for a moment, then turned to the monk and asked hesitantly, "We were told that in the early Ming Dynasty, Zhu Gong, King of Jin, came to Shaolin Temple."

"That's right," the monk nodded without any reluctance, "they lived here for six years and then left."

I think I must have looked ridiculously stunned. Even Seann sensed something unusual and didn't pressure me for an answer. The old monk was poised and collected, "The tablet remembering the King of Jin is up there," he said while calmly pointing to the rows of ebony tablets on the offering table. "We still pay homage to him along with all the other great masters of Shaolin."

I took a few deep breaths and turned around to relay the message to Seann. He paused for a moment, "Ask him if he knows where they went when they left?"

"Master, do you know where they went?"

"How would I know that? It was more than 600 years ago, and I am only 85 years old." He said with a smile.

I asked if we could take a picture of him with Seann, and he agreed. Before I could take the picture, some tourists walked up to the half open door and disturbed the old monk. I realized that we should probably leave and thanked him for spending time alone with us.

Seann and Shaolin Monk

Later in the evening, when we passed the ancestral hall after visiting some other touristy monuments, the door was closed again. We both had a feeling not many people are invited into the Ancestral Hall.

"They?" After we left Shaolin Temple and returned to the hotel, Seann asked, "Did he say if there were any other people besides Zhu Gong?"

"I didn't ask, but it makes sense for a territorial King to have an entourage." I replied.

"No, since he was trying not to be noticed, I don't think he would bring an entourage. There must had been someone very special with Zhu Gong."

"Then let's go back to Shaolin Temple tomorrow and ask him." I suggested, but he acted like he didn't hear me.

"Forget it, he may not be there." He closed his eyes and meditated for a while. When he opened his eyes, he asked me, "your Qigong teacher told you what happened in your lifetime 600 years ago, but she didn't mention Zhu Gong?"

"No, she was talking mainly about our life in the Palace of King of Chen. I told you already!"

"I don't remember, tell me again."

"She said that I was a trouble maker who caused a lot of turmoil, so they had to abandon the Palace and fled Nanjing. Anyway, if it hadn't been for her husband in this life, who was my elder brother back then, and was too protective of me, they wouldn't have to suffer all those difficulties."

"Still a trouble maker." He smiled at me. Before I could reply, he murmured, "Nanjing?" He looked like he found a piece of a puzzle, and with some reserved excitement said, "Let's go to Nanjing."

Now, we are in Nanjing. Were the strange dreams I was having related to what happened 600 years ago?

If Shaolin Abbot Renshan Yi Gong was the Abbot of Taiyuan Shongshan Temple for ten years before he went to Shaolin, then his relationship with the King of Jin must have been very close. It would make sense if the King of Jin wanted to hide, he would go to Shaolin. But why?

"Do you think it's possible the Abbot didn't die during his visit to Beijing, as the official history says, but was killed for protecting Zhu Gong?" Seann was deep in thought.

"Maybe." I had the same feeling after reading that. "I think Zhu Di probably found out Zhu Gong went to Shaolin, and was questioning the Abbot. But, there's no evidence. At most, we could say it's our opinion."

I can't find much information about the King of Jin on the Internet. All it says is that he died in 1398, and the cause of his death is vague. In Taiyuan, the historical Capital of the Jin territory, we went all over the place and tried to find the King's tomb, but found nothing.

The officially accepted history of the King of Jin does not make sense, and does not match what Ahtun Re said or the character of Seann. History is written by the winners. The possibility that Zhu Di changed the history and vilified Zhu Gong is, of course, very likely. It's just that, it's been more than 600 years, where can we find proof?

"There is no need for proof," Seann said calmly, "We know."

"So, are we still going to Yunnan?"

"Where do you think your Qigong teacher might be?"

"I think she's probably in Taipei."

"Then," he opened the laptop he had just closed, "Let's go to Taipei!"

REFERENCES

65. [Photo]
Shaolin Temple (Shaolin Temple, China)
intheeternal.com/en/id/466

66. [Link]
Da Guan Yuan : Wikipedia page
intheeternal.com/en/id/780

67. [Photo]
Shaolin Ancestral Hall (Shaolin Temple, China)
intheeternal.com/en/id/465

68. [Photo]
Seann and Shaolin Monk (Shaolin Temple, China)
intheeternal.com/en/id/463

10

Homeland

"We shall not cease from exploration,
And the end of all our exploring,
Will be to arrive where we started,
And know the place for the first time."

— T. S. Eliot

After leaving terminal 1 at Taoyuan Airport, I led Seann to the bus station and bought two tickets to Taipei. Since my parents moved to the US, I have always taken the Da-Yu bus to the Taipei Fu-Hua Hotel when I return to Taiwan.

I felt completely relaxed. It's so nice to be home!

I have lived in California for much longer than I lived in Taiwan, but Taiwan still feels like home.

I grew up in a countryside and loved it. While in college, I met a guy who grew up in a nearby farming community and talked about the bad things I did as a child, "Oh! You're one of them." He said, "My father hated those kids from your village. They were always making a mess in the vegetable fields, using the crops as toys, wasting food."

Yup! That was me, guilty as charged! Back then, everything was a free toy for us. The most expensive toy was about one yuan from me and 50 cents from my brother, to buy a Chinese chess set. Usually within a few days of playing, we would start fighting and accusing each other of cheating. Sometimes my mother would get tired of our quarrels and would tear up the paper chess board and

Yangmingshan, Taiwan

threw the wooden pieces into the garbage can. A couple of days later we made up, but our pockets were empty, so I would nudge my brother to go to my sister, who loves him dearly, to buy us another chess set to play.

My sister wrote in her book that when we were kids, my father was always overprotective of us. One night, we wanted to go with some older neighbor kids to the night market in town. My father forced us to put on tall rain boots because we had to walk through dark farmland. There were many snakes in the countryside and he was afraid that we could've been bitten. I put them on without any hesitation, but my sister refused to wear them because they were ugly. I didn't care, as long as we could go out to play.

"If you don't wear them, you're not allowed to go!" Father was very scary when he insisted on something. So she put them on obediently. Of course, we became the laughing stock of everyone. My sister wrote that she was embarrassed, but I responded to them, "So what, this way the snakes can't bite me!"

I don't know how young I was.

A similar story happened in my college freshman year. On winter break, I went to Alishan[71] with my classmates.

"It's cold on Alishan, the clothes you have are not enough!" When I was about to leave home, my father insisted on giving me his long trench coat.

On the night train up the mountain, I put on my father's trench coat to stay warm. A few of my classmates were whispering and laughing on the other side of the train car. My friend Luhwa told me, "They are laughing at you saying you look like a communist." At that moment, their comment bothered me. I couldn't be as free spirited as I had been when I was a child.

My father worked for the government, because of his position he had a government car and a driver. Sometimes, when I overslept, he would take a taxi to work, and had his driver drop me off at school so I wouldn't be late. I usually asked his driver drop me off a block or two from school, so that it looked like I took the bus, just like everyone else.

Unlike my conservative father, laid back and always with a book in his hand; my mother grew up in Shanghai, went to college in Japan, and was always outgoing and savvy. She often said, "Investing in the stock market is so easy, just buy low and sell high." What she didn't understand was that not every one had a good business sense like her. We wouldn't be able to attend graduate school in the States without her working two jobs and insisting to my father that women need to get a higher education, so we can be independent.

Every time I come back to Taiwan the memories of my childhood come back, but this time it seemed different. I began to appreciate the things that used to bother me, like my overprotective father, my nagging mother, the crowded buses of the city, and ...

"What are you thinking?" Seann brought me back to reality.

"Nothing, just some childhood memories." I started to tear up. "I wish I was a better daughter."

"Na... You weren't that bad." Obviously, he was trying to cheer me up. "You are you, I'm sure your parents love you for who you are."

"Thank you!" I said to him with gratefulness.

He nodded and suddenly took my hands in his. "I'm sorry for all the pressure I put on you in China."

I hesitated, and tried to choose my words carefully, "I should have known there would be a lot of unpredictable things happen along the way," he let go of my hands and I took a deep breathe, "so it's not entirely your fault."

He smiled, saying sarcastically, "Of course it's not my fault. How could I be at fault?" When I'm in a good mood, his sarcastic humor would make me laugh easily.

"I should take into consideration the impact that cultural differences might have on you." I said, "On top of the emotional impact of the feelings left over from the past, this trip is not just a sightseeing vacation, I should have planned it better before we left."

"I don't agree." He said, knowing I was in a good mood. "How much of what we've experienced could have been planned?"

"Okay, I agree with you about not using limited knowledge to plan for an infinite future, but I'm not used to this kind of directionless, wandering way." I protested.

"Not having a fixed direction means all directions are possible. Every successful exploration in life requires us to be open to the unknown," he said. "Only by letting go of the self-imposed limits we have accumulated over the years, maybe over many lifetimes, can we allow possibilities that we cannot imagine into our experience. We need to have a rough idea of where we are going, but stay open to possibilities that we didn't know existed, so when they show up we pay attention."

"Yeah, but I do think that more preparation and planning can reduce the chance of unexpected obstacles." I retorted.

"There's an old saying," he always like to present a different view, "when a man or woman...," he smiled, knowing that equality is important to me, "are making plans, God is laughing up there. We have such a limited perspective, and yet we act as if we know the best way."

His lighthearted confidence reminded me of a Buddhist saying, "Let go, have faith that Buddha will be there for you even if you have to jump off cliff..." Can all these be considered tests and trials that we need to go through?

"You know what?" He continued, "Sometimes we have to hit our head against the wall, before realizing that the answer was right in front of us all along. If we didn't try, we would not realize it. So, we learn one way or another..."

"I have been searching for you in the crowd
A thousand times around,
Suddenly, I turned,
And there you are,
Just standing right there,
Under the shadowy lights."

I recited the poem[72] by Xin Qiji. He looked at me confused. So I explained.

"You really know a lot. I am impressed."

"It's such a famous poem, everyone knows it by heart." I responded, forgetting for a moment that Seann is American.

"Really?"

"I told you that I hated memorization and didn't like going to school. It's a miracle that I survived Taiwan's education system. I was lucky."

"No, I bet it's because you were cute and teachers gave you preferential treatment."

"Yeah... Maybe..." I remembered most of my middle school teachers were my mom's colleagues and our neighbors, so they had seen me grow up in that teachers' village.

"Actually, I had ADD when I was young. I just didn't realize it until I saw how my students would struggle."

"Yup, I have noticed that."

"Noticed what?"

"Your ADD." He said, half jokingly.

I shrugged it off. "I told my students that if I made it, they could all do better."

"Did they believe you?"

"No, not really." I shook my head. "But some were more willing to try and make improvements, enough to pass Algebra and graduate from high school."

"But, you also gave too much of your energy to your students. That's why your health suffered during those years, and that is why you burned out and left." he said, knowing I quit because of health issues.

"Yeah, but it was worth it." I said, proudly. "All the thank you notes, Christmas cards, and the prom pictures... I still have them. One time, a student ran across the parking lot to give me a hug. A good teacher can really make a difference, and they appreciated that."

Seann nodded.

"But seriously, I was a terrible student. I remember when we were studying Geometry, and I couldn't get it. My sister was so patient, she went over one question 11 times with me, and it finally clicked. Since then Geometry became my strongest subject."

"I hated Geometry."

"Well, that's because you didn't have a sister that went over the same question 11 times with you." We looked at each other and laughed quietly, not wanting to disturb passengers who were trying to nap on the long late night drive.

I breathed a sigh of relief as the lights of downtown Taipei were getting closer. And suddenly out of nowhere, I remembered the first time I left Taiwan to attend graduate school in the States.

My father never took advantage of his position for personal benefit, but that day he did. He used his privileged status as a high ranking government official, to escort me and my sister all the way to the airplane door.

As I stepped onto the empty Boeing 747, I realized that I would not be able to come home for a long time. Just as I turned around to say goodbye to my father, he was wiping tears from his eyes...

We never discussed love in our household. But, in that moment, I realized that my dad loved us, even though he had never said those words.

REFERENCES

69. [Photo]
Yangmingshan View (Yangmingshan, Taiwan)
intheeternal.com/en/id/619

70. [Photo]
Yangmingshan Field (Yangmingshan, Taiwan)
intheeternal.com/en/id/486

71. [Link]
Alishan Scenic Area : Wikipedia page
intheeternal.com/en/id/781

72. [Link]
Xin Qiji Poem : Website
intheeternal.com/en/id/782

11

The Unseen

"Magic is real. Let's deal with it."

— Dean Radin

My life had been extremely busy for many years. Between my work, building a house, plus my daughters' sporting activities, I hardly had any time for myself. After my youngest daughter Yuan-Yuan went to the same university with her sister, Xiang-Xiang, I finally got to relax and enjoy what I truly wanted to do.

On top of the interesting books I found at the book store, I also spent days and evenings watching interviews with leading scientists and philosophers about spirituality, social and climate issues, and other more esoteric subjects. Some documentaries also caught my attention, and the wealth of information was overwhelming.

Years later Seann and I had a conversation about our interest in metaphysical subjects, and what we had learned. From our perspective as former technology professionals, metaphorically each individual person is like a computer without Internet access; we have limited capabilities and knowledge. However, if we connect to the Internet, then we can receive unimaginable, limitless information, and download additional functionality. The problem is, there is too much noise and distraction on the Internet, and we have to learn to distinguish between the true and helpful, versus the untrue and unhelpful. Connecting and tuning into the higher spiritual realms to access information, requires wisdom and discernment, just like using the internet, otherwise we can be misled.

In recent years there is increasing interest among everyday people in subjects like quantum physics and multi-dimensional reality, and organizations like the Institute of Noetic Sciences (IONS)[74] and the Monroe Institute[75] have been researching subjects such as psychic abilities and other so-called paranormal phenomena for many decades. Dr. Dean Radin[76], Chief Scientist at IONS, has published over 300 articles and many books, primarily exploring the nature of non-local consciousness.

So, while some of the things we discuss in this chapter may seem strange to some people, they are increasingly being recognized as real and measurable phenomena. Science is finally catching up...

— 今 —

More than twenty years ago I began to practice Qigong, after a car accident caused persistent back pain. No matter what kind of doctor I went to, Eastern or Western, no treatment could make the pain go away. I did not want to spend the rest of my life taking pain medicine, so I finally asked my friend to introduce me to my Qigong teacher. After the first session, I was smiling because all my pain subsided.

My Qigong teacher, Jennifer, said I was her second worst student. Her husband, Thomas, was the worst. After we knew each other for a few years, knowing how lazy I could be, she moved the Qigong class to my backyard thinking it would force me to practice. But when all the students had arrived, sometimes I was still sleeping.

Later they moved to the Malibu waterfront, and I had to drive over an hour to her apartment to practice. At that point I started to take it more seriously, but truthfully, it was probably my love for the beach that inspired my renewed enthusiasm for practice.

Land of Medicine Buddha

One weekend I went with Jennifer and Thomas to teach Qigong at the Land of Medicine Buddha Retreat in Santa Cruz. During the lunch break, a Taoist friend from Taiwan was talking about his struggle with various health issues over the years. Being a foolishly kindhearted person, I was very sympathetic with him. But Jennifer gave me a wink, and finally got up and pulled me away from the table. After the afternoon class ended, Thomas and Jennifer hurriedly packed their bags and started the drive back to Los Angeles, without stopping.

Thomas was driving the van, and I was sleeping on the back row of chairs. There was a sense of uneasiness from Jennifer and Thomas, but I was tired and soon fell asleep. I didn't know how long it had been, but when I woke up from my sleep, I was a little disoriented. The strange dream I just had was still so vivid.

I got up, moved to the front of the van and sat down behind Jennifer. Thomas looked back at me and said, "Good for you. You can still sleep at this time." His tone was relaxed and the uneasiness I had felt earlier was gone.

"I just had a weird dream."

"What was the weird dream?" Jennifer turned back to me, with a curious look on her face.

"I dreamt of many weird-looking...ghosts, I guess. They were lined up in front of our van with all kinds of weapons...."

"And, what happened?" She looked concerned.

"I jumped out and fought with them!"

"Oh." she laughed, "You fought them off?"

Before I could answer, Thomas added, "There were a bunch of ghosts behind the guy you were talking with at lunch."

"Really?" I asked, surprised.

"Yes, really. I was feeling nauseous, but you kept talking with him," Jennifer said. "Our energy helped him, so he kept talking to us. But, the ghosts who were feeding off his negative energy were not happy that we helped him, and they wanted to cause some trouble for us. Luckily, you have good Qi and were able to chase them away."

"Otherwise, I would still be worried about getting into an accident." Thomas interjected. "We both were feeling more relaxed just a little earlier, but didn't know why."

"Really?" I asked again, still taking in the story they were explaining to me.

"Really. You have good energy, but you must practice Qi Gong. You need to be more aware, so you know how to avoid situations like that...at least you have to be more careful when I'm not around." Jennifer said, smiling.

Twenty years later, after experiencing countless challenges, I finally understand her advice. Unfortunately, back then I was young and busy, and besides meditation, I hardly had time to practice much of what I learned.

— 今 —

In March of 2001, I was in Chicago at a training program. During a break, I called home and Yuan-Yuan answered the phone, "Mommy, I'm hungry" she complained.

"Go ask grandma for food, ok?" I tried to comfort her.

"Nobody's home, they all went to the hospital."

I booked the next flight home, knowing something was very wrong. When I stepped into the ICU, although my father[78] was unconscious, his vital signs went crazy. A nurse ran into the room to check on him, asking me, "What's going on?" When she couldn't find anything wrong, she left baffled. He never regained conscious, and I regretted not taking the time to tell him that I love him.

Originally, the hospital told us to prepare for the funeral, but my father's condition had improved over the following weeks. So, they asked us to find a nursing home for him because he needed continuous care.

I sat with him in the ICU before flying out for work on Sunday night. I held his hand and told him not to worry about me. I knew he was unhappy when I got divorced, worried that nobody would be around to take care of me. "I don't want you to suffer, dad." I told him, and saw his face moved a little. "Don't worry about me. I have a good job, I will be fine. You don't need to stay, you don't need to suffer."

The following Wednesday, I received a message from my sister that he had passed. The earliest flight back to LA I could find was in the next morning. That night, I cried myself to sleep in the hotel.

Vividly, in a dream I saw my father brought two
Angelic looking beings with him to visit me. "Shhh,"
he told them, "don't wake her up, she's sleeping." I
noticed both of those beings had blue eyes.

When I returned home, the large flower basket sent by my boss stood quietly in front of the door. I put down my luggage, carried the flower basket into the living room, sat down, covered my face and cried bitterly.

"Mei-Mei ...." Suddenly, my father's voice rang through my consciousness. I stopped crying, wiped my tears, and tried to calm myself down. I noticed a faint scent of sandalwood in the air.

"Mei-Mei ...." Father called me again. I lowered my head and listened attentively. "Don't cry. Dad is fine." Tears started flowing uncontrollably. I knew he would be okay, but I was still sad.

In the days that followed, communication between my father and me became a regular part of my life. And it wasn't just me, my sister, brother, and nephew all had their own telepathic interaction with my father after he died.

Over the years, I have learned that communication with the spirit world varies from person to person. It may be due to the fact that everyone has different beliefs, expectations, and perception. To me, it seemed my father was much more light hearted and playful, wise and humorous. Like an anchor and a steering wheel, he guided me through that turbulent period of my life. He told me many things, including that my mother would be leaving us in five months.

My mother's attachment to the physical world was too tenacious and insistent. Although she believed in Christianity, she had no understanding or interest in the supernatural or spiritual world. Father was concerned that her transition to the other side would be difficult. That's why he stayed around, he seemed to be waiting, so he could help her when the time came.

In October, autumn gradually covered everything in colors. My mother, who was always passionate about learning, had started taking English classes at the local adult school. My mother's energy, complexion, and mood were improving everyday. She would walk from my brother's house to the bus stop whenever I wasn't able to drive her. But, I hadn't forgotten what my father told me, that one thing I really didn't want to believe. I asked my father if he was mistaken. He did not answer me.

One day I had to attend a meeting, and couldn't go pick up mother from her school. When I walked out of that meeting, the clear deep blue sky was getting dark, with colorful glow emanating from behind the mountainside. Looking at the beautiful autumn sunset, I felt a little uneasy, and had the urge to rush home as soon as possible. I was about to leave when my phone rang,

"Mommy, Ger-Ger (my nephew) called and said grandma's in the hospital."

My mother had a massive stroke while going home from English class, and died in the hospital a few days later. Even though my father had told me way in advance that she would pass soon, it was still very difficult for me to accept. After my mother's funeral, I sensed that they had left together. Since then, my father stopped communicating with me and I only see them in my dreams occasionally.

The conscious exchange with my father in those days proved one thing to me, "love" does not die at the end of the physical life. Whenever we remember them, we could always sense their love and presence in our heart.

Los Angeles County, California
March 2010

In the spring of 2010, Xiang-Xiang decided to join the Los Angeles Marathon on a whim. My ex-husband, Dr. Chen, was very nervous and gave me a hard time.

"A marathon is not like a basketball game, 26.5 miles (42.4 km), it's not a joke."

What can I do when my daughter made up her mind?

Early that morning, after dropping off Xiang-Xiang at Dodger Stadium, Dr. Chen bought breakfast and woke everyone up. He was tracking his daughter's progress on his laptop. While keeping an eye on her, he pushed us to get ready so we could leave early and wait for her at the finish line in Santa Monica.

It was still pretty chilly at Santa Monica beach front in spring. The sea breeze was blowing, and Yuan-Yuan, my niece and I were huddled together to keep each other warm. Dr. Chen was walking around, like an eagle, watching the runners coming down the street.

Finally, Dr. Chen rushed over to us and said, "Xiang-Xiang is here!" Then he turned around and ran down the street, forgetting the normally reserved demeanor of a professor and senior Fellow Engineer, shouting out to the group of runners, "Xiang-Xiang, daddy's here, and mommy's over there!" He pointed at us.

She didn't even look at him, and just kept running. "Save your breath," I said to Dr. Chen, "She can't hear you."

"Hold this." He handed me his computer bag, "I'll go find her."

When we arrived home, Xiang-Xiang used her last bit of strength to climb up stairs. She couldn't even reach her own room, grabbed me and fell asleep on my bed. I used Qigong to massage her muscles and bones through out her body, and then fell asleep also.

Since I learned Qigong, for almost twenty years, I was able to help the girls so they hardly had any illness. Occasional sports injuries could also be healed quickly. But, I underestimated the power of the marathon.

I woke up to a phone call when it was dark. The house was unusually quiet, and Xiang-Xiang disappeared from the bed. I reached out for my cell phone, but found my arm was not moving as directed. On the other end of the line came Seann's worried voice.

"Are you okay? I've called a few times and you didn't pick up."

"I'm sorry, I was sleeping. I'm probably a little sick from the cold ocean breeze."

"I'm going out to get food, so don't worry about making dinner, get some rest."

I sat up and tried to get out of bed, but found that my whole body was extremely sore. Slowly, step by step, holding on to the hand rail, I walked down the stairs. Shortly after I sat down at the breakfast table, Seann came in with dinner. It didn't take long for me to get really tired, I couldn't even finish the food.

"I've never seen you sick before. How did you get so sick from just the sea breeze?" Seann asked.

"It's okay, I'll go get some sleep, I'll be fine tomorrow."

But tomorrow was even worse.

My head was heavy, my whole body was almost paralyzed, and I couldn't get out of bed.

""Marathons are overrated!" Xiang-Xiang came in, pointed to the phone in her hand, and whispered to me, "Bo-Bo" (my oldest daughter's nick name) then she lied down next to me, and continued talking to her sister.

"Those people must have trained wrong. I've only been training for three months and ran easily, without a hitch. I even went to the beach campfire last night with my high school classmates... okay, I have to go pack, Yuan-Yuan has been bugging me the whole morning already. Here's mommy." She handed her phone to me.

"Mom, Xiang-Xiang says you're sick?" Bo-Bo asked, concerned.

"I don't know what's wrong. I don't have any other symptoms, just aches and pains, and I can hardly move."

"Ha! I know what's wrong. You took on all those aches and pains from Xiang-Xiang. Maybe it's not that others don't know how to train, but they don't have a mother who knows Qigong."

The girls went back to Santa Barbara, and I was sick for a week.

Seann brought me tea, water, and food every day. After a few days he finally moved me to the guest house so he could take care of me. When I thanked him, he joked, "No problem, that is why I am here."

When I didn't laugh he said, "My award winning sense of humor is not working today."

Then, I laughed.

That first year together wasn't easy, and we did not always get along. But the one thing that was becoming more clear, was that we both really care about each other.

— 今 —

On one of our morning coffee talks, Seann's aura was unusually bright, his eyes were sparkling also.

"I haven't told you this before..." he paused, "Hans Christian King[79], back around 2005, told me I am a medium. He also said I am a healer."

"You told me you had sessions with him, but you haven't mentioned the medium part." I said, wondering why he was bringing it up now.

"I wasn't sure if you were comfortable with the idea, so I didn't mention it. The healer part makes sense. I took Reiki classes when I first moved to Austin, and when practicing, the teacher said he hadn't experienced such strong energy from a student before."

I nodded. There are times I felt strong energy from Seann also.

"The medium part I wasn't comfortable with for a long time, so when he brought up the subject I would try to talk about something else. He said that if I decided to develop it, I could help heal people through writing. I had never considered writing to be a form of healing, but the way he explained it, actually made sense."

He paused for a few seconds, as if to make sure it was okay to tell me the next part, then continued.

"About a year before we met, I flew to Asheville to take one of his mediumship development classes. That is the first time I met Hans in person.

He was taller than me, a large broad shouldered man, which was interesting considering how kind and gentle he was on the phone. On the last day of the course, standing by the entrance of the meeting facility and away from the rest of the class participants, he put his hand on my heart and said that I had been hurt in another lifetime. And that to him it felt like a lump of coal in my heart chakra. He said I needed to heal my heart."

He looked away, but I could see he was getting a little emotional.

"That is why I went to North Carolina to write, I had been there for his class, and liked the mountains."

"I wondered about that. That makes sense."

"Yeah, it made sense at the time. But after we met I realized two things. One, without what we have learned this last year exploring our past, anything I wrote would not have been complete. There was a lot I didn't understand back then, especially about reincarnation."

"Yeah, me too." I added agreeably.

I was waiting for the second thing, but he was staring off into the distance. Finally I asked, "And what was the second thing you realized?"

"I realized, that the lump of coal in my heart, the thing that kept me from getting into serious relationships, and that made me downplay the importance of love...was related to the pain of the past. Our past. That was a very difficult life...for both of us."

I felt astonished by his realization.

"It's not related to something from my childhood, or some traumatic event in this life. It was from another lifetime. How could I have known that, if we didn't meet and go through this process?"

"Well, I guess that's why we met." I tried to ease the emotional vulnerability caused by learning about our past life involvement.

"And that's the way it is for a lot of people. They are carrying emotional pain, or self-imposed limitations, that have nothing to do with their current life experience. But, it also works the other way too." He said, looking more positive.

"What do you mean?"

"Well, I visited Chinatown for herbs and used the I-Ching when I was 20. I am a white guy from Texas, that is not a part of my culture. I have probably also been a monk before, that's why I like reading metaphysical books, and don't mind being alone. It's all part of my soul memory, things that carried over from previous lifetimes. It's the same with you too," he said, smiling.

"You talked before about healing your kids when they were injured. Not everyone can do that. And you also, like your dad, aren't chasing after money. That's probably because you have been wealthy before, and you know that's not the answer you were seeking."

"Yeah, but being wealthy had a lot of advantages too." I said in protest.

"True, it can. But it can also be a big burden. I learned that after all of those years working for very wealthy people."

"I believe that."

"Anyway, the point is, we are who we are and know what we know because of who we have been before. I didn't get that before we met. But now, a lot of things make much more sense. And, it also means that if we work on ourselves, and clear our karma and become better people in this life, in our next life we might be able to start off from a better place. It could be much easier next time."

"I am not coming back." I said, still protesting. "This is not a nice place."

"But, if we could remember all of these things when we are young in the next lifetime, we could have an amazing life. You could miss out with that kind of attitude."

"I don't care. I just wanted to focus on here and now," I responded with my typical defiant temperament.

But he was right in many ways. Each lifetime we learn, build, and grow; and eventually all of our efforts accumulate into the life we live today. And, what we do now determines what kind of life we will have in our future lifetimes. It is like what Buddhism says,

> *"If you want to know what have you done in your*
> *past life, reflect on what's happening in your current*
> *life. If you want to know the future of your next*
> *life, look at what you are doing in this life."*

REFERENCES

73. [Photo]
    The Unseen (Hsi Lai Temple, California)
    intheeternal.com/en/id/818

74. [Link]
    IONS : Institute of Noetic Sciences
    intheeternal.com/en/id/784

75. [Link]
    Monroe Institute : Website
    intheeternal.com/en/id/785

76. [Note]
    Dr. Dean Radin : About
    intheeternal.com/en/id/524

77. [Photo]
    Land of Medicine Buddha (Santa Cruz, California)
    intheeternal.com/en/id/434

78. [Note]
    PoTa Chou : About
    intheeternal.com/en/id/531

79. [Note]
    Hans Christian King : About
    intheeternal.com/en/id/528

12

Synchronicity

*"The concept of synchronicity
indicates a meaningful coincidence
of two or more events,
where something other than the
probability of chance is involved."*

— Carl G. Jung

Los Angeles County, California
November 2010

After living in my guest house for almost a year, Seann asked me to move to Northern California with him. He suggested that by moving someplace new, we can open ourselves to new possibilities.

We talked about it after attending a Qigong workshop in San Diego. "For you to stay in a situation where you just water the plants, wash the dishes and take out the trash is just... that's not an effective use of your abilities. The kids are in college and are old enough to take care of themselves now."

"Yeah." I had to agree. But there was the practical side of me that resisted.

"Once you make a decision to do something, a way will be made. Things show up. We just have to take the first step." In the end, basically he just asked me to have faith.

"When we were at Land of Medicine Buddha, walking through the pine forest, I found you a 4 leaf clover. I will find a way to make this happen. It's time."

We made several trips to northern California, and we both liked North Bay the most. When Seann found a cute garden villa in Santa Rosa, I finally opened up to the possibility.

Santa Rosa-Deck

Then, out of no where, one of his old clients called. They asked him to fly to Montana for an electronics project, which helped pay for six months at the garden villa.

"What do we do after six months?" I was still not sure if I should give up everything. I had been living in that area of LA county for over twenty years. Friends and family were all firmly tied to the area.

"More possibilities will show up," he said, "You just need to let old habits and routines fall away, to allow space for new things to happen." As it turned out, he did get more calls for programming work, and I learned to have more faith.

I have experienced many similar situations in my life. That is also the way Seann came into my chaotic life, without any warning and outside of all my conscious plans. His appearance made huge waves, and forced me to face things that I did not want to face, like the shadows of my previous incarnations causing emotional blockages in my present life.

Of course, what I didn't understand was that as long as there's any unresolved psychological shadows, it's difficult for us to achieve true peace of mind.

Los Angeles County, California
July 2009

On July 14, 2009, I got back home from Santa Barbara, exhausted from dealing with my two daughters' housing arrangement for the next school year. I was so tired that I couldn't sleep, as the dream I had that morning was replaying in front of my eyes like a video.

In my dream, I opened a metal gate and walked into the garden. On each side of the path was a row of cylindrical drums. At the end of the path was a large Buddha with flowers and fruits in front of it.

Tashi Choling - Oregon

*I knelt down and bowed three times. Then I got up
and walked to the left side, which was dedicated to
another Buddha. I bowed three times again. When I
got up, I saw a plaque fallen in the lotus pond. I
picked it up from the water and saw the sign saying,
"White Tara". I put the sign down, but it fell into the
pond again. At that time, I saw that there was a pink
glass bead in the place where I had put the sign.*

"It's for you."

*An incredibly kind voice rang in my ears. I
reached out and picked up the glass bead and saw
pink, gold, and white lights beaming out of it.*

*"Your love and kindness, like the lights
of this bead, will not be ignored."*

*I looked up, a white golden light shining out
of White Tara covering my whole body.*

*"From today on, you have to take care of
yourself more. Don't cancel your trip..."*

Then, my daughter's phone call woke me up.

In May, I asked Xiang-Xiang's permission to take her to a spiritual workshop in Los Angeles, thinking it might help her. But, the day before the class, she disappeared and wouldn't return my calls. At first I was angry because I was doing this for her, but after I calmed down, I decided to go by myself.

I learned a lot from the two-day course, and was glad I went. After the class, I asked the teachers' secretary to see if I could get a refund for my daughter's tuition. They offered two options, either a refund, or I could apply it towards the tuition for the next level workshop, in Albuquerque. At that point, I was very impressed with the two teachers, so I paid the small difference to register for the next workshop.

The high energy I received in the class did not last long, and was soon dissipated by the mundane responsibilities of my life. In the following days, I was busy handling my daughters' summer plans, arranging the next school year's housing, and budgeting the cost of them traveling around the world with the "Semester at Sea" program. I was so exhausted, I had already thinking that maybe I should cancel the Albuquerque trip.

As I laid in bed, reflecting on the very clear message delivered in the dream I had that morning, and decided to give myself a vacation. I got up, turned on my computer, and booked a hotel in Sedona and Albuquerque. It was decided, I was going. I breathed a sigh of relief, and finally fell into sleep.

Sara in Sedona

Sedona, Arizona
July 2009

The next evening, in a dusty and unpretentious manner, I arrived at Sedona, a popular spiritual center in Northern Arizona. Under the moonless night, those magnificent red rocks were scarcely visible.

After settling in the hotel, I picked up a travel brochure on the coffee table. It read:

> Francesca,
> You asked me about the interesting places to visit
> around here, and I highly recommend 'Huck'. He is a
> great guide and knows the vortexes of Sedona area
> very well. I promise you won't be disappointed!
> Love, Sara

On the reverse side was a photograph of an indigenous looking man with long black hair, playing a flute, and wearing red native clothing. His name, Huck, and contact number were written below the photo.

The name "Francesca" was the English name I used those years. The strange thing was that I booked the reservation online, and didn't ask anyone about vortexes.

It wasn't until I was sorting through my things before moving to Northern California that I saw the brochure again, and realized that there's much bigger plan at play. "Sara" was the name I started to use about a year after the Albuquerque workshop. That's why I didn't pay attention to who it was from at the time.

Psychologist Carl Jung first introduced the theory of Synchronicity in the 1920s. In short, when a series of synchronistic coincidences occur in our lives, it is often interpreted as an indication that we are going in the right direction, aligning with our life's purpose.

James Redfield brought the theory of synchronicity into the public consciousness in his best-selling novel, The Celestine Prophecy[84]. He argued that all "coincidences" have significant meaning that cannot be ignored. For they point the way, leading us to, and unlocking the purpose and true meaning of life.

Some describe synchronicity as good fortune knocking on their door, or pointing to their destiny. Others see synchronicity as a miracle, or divine intervention, etc.

According to some spiritual teachings, meditation, contempla-
tion, prayer, and other practices that explore the deeper level of
our consciousness can sometimes deliberately provoke certain synchronicity.

That night, in the Sedona hotel, I was holding the travel
brochure in my hand and flipping through it, wondering what it
was trying to show me. What I didn't realize was that it was just
the first wink from the Universe, and that there were many more
synchronistic events waiting for me.

REFERENCES

80. [Photo]
Forest (Santa Cruz, California)
intheeternal.com/en/id/831

81. [Photo]
Santa Rosa Deck (Santa Rosa, California)
intheeternal.com/en/id/441

82. [Image]
Tashi Choling
intheeternal.com/en/id/512

83. [Photo]
Sara in Sedona (Sedona, Arizona)
intheeternal.com/en/id/431

84. [Book]
Redfield, J. (1993) The Celestine Prophecy
intheeternal.com/en/id/816

13

Soul Mates

On the way to Albuquerque I passed the Meteor Crater in Northern Arizona. I wasn't in a hurry, and couldn't resist my curiosity, so I took the next exit and turned around to go see it. It was a dusty, hot day, and when getting back in my truck to leave I had a sunburn and a lot of dust on my face from walking around the crater. I also lingered too long, which delayed my trip. When I finally arrived in Albuquerque on the evening of the 17th, I didn't have time to get out my luggage, so I went straight to the hotel ballroom where the workshop was taking place, to check in.

I was wearing a sporting skort, tank top, a messy hairdo, and was covered with dust. When I walked into the ballroom lobby I was still carrying the high energy from my stay in Sedona and visiting the Crater. There were three men sitting on the couch in the lounge, and all of them turned to look at me. One of them got up and walked over to chat with me. I thought to myself, "That's weird, look at me. How could I attract strangers' attention?" I wasn't in a social mood, and just wanted to finish the paperwork and go back to my room to wash up and get some rest.

"Cell phone?" The assistant teacher, who had also been at the Los Angeles event, handed me a plastic bag.

I flinched and instinctively replied, "I don't have it."

"Then please go back and get it. Everyone has to check-in their cellphone until Sunday, so we stay focused on the energy of the event," he said.

My good mood immediately turned into a cloud of smoke. I turned around, left the line of people, and went back to my room feeling agitated.

"What the ..." I thought to myself, "My daughter calls me every night." I was cursing in my mind when the phone rang.

After ending the phone call with my daughter I looked at the time, there was only five more minutes before the class started. I sat quietly for a few moments then decided that if they insisted to take my phone, I will not attend the class.

When I returned to the check in lobby, the long table had already been removed. There was only one small table and a red-haired assistant teacher who I hadn't seen before.

"Register?" She smiled at me, saying, "here...sign here," then handed me a folder with class materials.

I exhaled, grabbed my folder and walked fast toward the conference hall.

"Wait, wait." She suddenly stood up and called out to me. "You are Francesca?"

"Yes."

"This one is for you. Can I have that folder back?"

I rolled my eyes and thought to myself, "Why do they have a folder just for me?" Frustrated with the cell phone comment, and being given a different folder, I walked into the ballroom almost disenchanted. As events unfolded over the next few days, I learned how wrong my preconceived notions were.

Usually, when we are unhappy because of other's words or actions, it is likely that we have those thoughts in our own mind. Maybe it is a lack of self-confidence, or a biased wrong perception, or just a simple prejudice. In short, I have learned that everything we see outside is a projection of our own inner world.

Seann almost gave up attending the workshop after the same assistant asked for his cellphone. He questioned their policy, and even though they said it would be stored in the hotel office safe, he couldn't take the chance of it being misplaced. He also might need to be able to return emergency calls from his clients.

He told the assistant he needed to think about it, and left the check-in line. After going back to his room and contemplating the situation, he decided to lock it in the safe in his room. If they didn't agree to let him keep it there, he was going to leave Albuquerque.

When he arrived at the Albuquerque airport the previous evening, the red-haired assistant teacher who checked me in, was waiting outside for the hotel shuttle. With her flowing white dress and calm centered demeanor, Seann thought she might be attending the same workshop. He introduced himself and asked her, which turned into a conversation that lasted until they arrived at the hotel.

Her father was a doctor in the Netherlands, and she had an interest in nutrition and alternative healing techniques since she was young. Volunteering for the event would allow her to get exposure to the energy healing techniques they were teaching. And, over the next several days it was obvious to both of us that while she was new to the material, she carried the energy of an experienced healer.

Seann went back to register just after the event had started, probably 10 minutes after me, and she was still at the registration desk. After a brief chat she pointed to the folders left on the registration desk, and asked him to pick one. And, she did not ask about his cell phone either.

When we later recalled the events that led to us meeting, I would joke that he had chosen me. And, this mysterious Dutch lady had unknowingly facilitated the whole thing...

— ⇡ —

The first day of the intensive class passed quickly. There were a few older men in the class that seemed pretty interested in me. I told them that I was single and had been divorced for many years, but was not interested in a relationship and did not want to get married again. Later, we learned that one of the advertised benefits of the course was to help people find their "soul mate." Seann and I, both from the technology world, were not into the idea of soul mates, but we were interested in the energy healing material. And, both of us questioned our decision to attend the event, at least until the second evening.

The second day at lunch, Marco, who was particularly nice to me, came and sat next to me again. People were talking about going to a Mexican restaurant for dinner. Lunch was vegetarian and included in the tuition, but some people were not used to eating vegetarian food. When everyone had decided on that restaurant, Marco turned to me and asked, "Are you going too?"

"I'm vegetarian."

"I heard the vegetarian food is excellent there also." Arturo said enthusiastically, "Really, let's go, I will drive."

In that high-energy space, even an anti-social person like me couldn't say no.

After the lunch break, I went back to class. The teaching assistants had lined up chairs facing each other in two long rows. As soon as I sat down, Marco, always nearby, grabbed the seat across from me.

At the beginning of the class, the teacher asked us to take the "Bindi" (a little round raised button with a colorful pattern on the front and adhesive on the back) out of the binder and give it to our partner, to help stick it to the center of our foreheads.

I mindlessly put mine on Marco's forehead, "No, no!" the red-haired assistant teacher rushed to stop me. "That's yours. You're going to help Marco put his on, and Marco will help you put yours on."

I thought, "It's just a bindi, what's all the fuss?"

The next step was to stand up and go find the person who has a bindi with the same design as ours. Apparently there were only two of the same design, so there were only two people with the same bindi.

The bindi was on my forehead, how would I know what it looks like? How could I find someone who has the same bindi as mine? The strange thing was that no one seemed to have the problem I had. Many of them were finding their partners very quickly, and were chatting joyously already. I wandered around looking for an opportunity to sneak out of the room. Maybe I could go take a nap... skipping class was my specialty in my school years.

But before I could act, Seann appeared, looking at me with a gentlemanly smile. I gave him a look and thought, "It can't be him...what do we have in common?" But he stood there quietly, smiling at me.

"Are we...do we have the same bindi?" I reached over to a teaching assistant I met in Los Angles, and pointed to Seann. She looked back at him, startled, and said without any hesitation, "I don't think so."

I breathed a sigh of relief and was about to sneak out as I had planned, but the red-haired assistant teacher came over to check on me. Seann was still standing there, a little baffled. So I asked her, "Do we have the same bindi?"

"Let me look...yes, you're the same. Now, find a set of open chairs where you can talk. In about 30 minutes we will have the final session for the day." Neither Seann or I really understood the exercise, we only knew that we were supposed to have something in common. We looked around and saw everyone sitting and talking, I pointed to a far corner and said, "Let's go there."

We actually did have a lot in common, and ended up talking at every break and at every meal, until the last afternoon, when Seann almost missed his flight, because we were still talking.

Later, I asked Seann how he found out about the workshop, and how he found me? He said that one of the two bindi's in the binder was supposed to be put on our forehead the first night of the class. He missed that part of the introduction, so there was an extra one in the binder he could look at. That's how he found me.

Seann's story leading up to the event was a little more complicated than mine. In February he flew to Burbank to attend an expo hosted by George Noory, where he met these spiritual teachers. Then, he booked this workshop after the Burbank event, thinking it might provide some good material for his book.

He rented a log cabin in the Smokey Mountains of North Carolina, and was already packed and ready to go, planning to leave after he returned to Austin. His plan was to write a book detailing what he had learned during the past 20 years of spiritual practice and research. But, neither of us knew that we would meet. Still unsure of what it all meant, after that weekend event, we would both go back to our lives...or so we thought.

The four hour drive to Sedona from Albuquerque was like a waking dream. Images were flowing in and out of my awareness, so vivid, sometimes even with sound and dialogue. It was like watching a movie. One image followed another, like a non-stop revolving lantern with a different scene in each turn. I wondered, was that our past life?

I arrived after the hotel was already closed. There was a letter on the office door that said, "I think you'll want to stay in the same room, the key is in the mailbox. Have good dreams! See you in the morning."

After washing off my fatigue, I sat down on the bed. Looking over toward the coffee table, Huck's brochure was still lying there. I shook my head gently, let out a long sigh and got up to put the brochure into my purse.

Huck is indeed a good tour guide. A few days ago, when I stayed here on the way to Albuquerque, he took me and two ladies from Italy on a tour of Sedona in his Jeep. He explained that each vortex emits different energies. Water is feminine and rocks are masculine. After visiting the feminine vortex by the river, he took us to the masculine vortex up on the Airport Mesa, so that balance could be achieved.

Reflecting on my trip, and happy to be back in Sedona, I laid down and closed my eyes. The sound of Huck's drum and flute seemed to be still playing in my ears.

"You must write your story, it will help many people understand that death is not the end and birth is not the beginning......"

It was a sweet feminine voice that interrupted the music, very clear and powerful. Was that the voice of the White Tara? It didn't matter. The sound of Huck's drum and flute, together with the sweet desert air outside coming thru the window, accompanying me as I drifted further and further away into my dreamland.

The next day, continuing the drive back to Los Angeles, I traveled through a little mountain town named Jerome, hanging on several thousand feet high cliffs. "Am I ready?" I asked myself. "Do I trust destiny enough that I could jump off that high cliff and the Great Spirit will catch me?"

After returning home to my old life, things were the same, even though I felt different. Nevertheless, I wasn't ready to seriously consider what I had been shown. So I kept all the realizations to myself, sent my best wishes to Seann, and decided to let the past go. "At least I know he's doing well," I rationalized to myself.

I could pretend that nothing important had happened and go back to sleep; go back to the comfort of old habits. Yes, that's what I was going to do.

End of story.

Or not. A few nights later I had another lucid dream...

> Seann and I were walking in a curved white corridor, his arm resting on my shoulder, and my left hand on his lower back. He was in pain, and I was trying to help him. There were other people walking with us, talking with Seann. He was wearing a white robe. Actually, I was wearing a white robe also. Everyone was wearing white. Everything was white.

> We stopped on a hill and were looking out over the city. The whole city is built along side small hills, with low single-story white buildings stretching all the way to the sea. Far in the distance, sea water was coming in...

> Seann was busy directing people to evacuate. He was still in pain, but he ordered me to leave. There was one seat on the last flying ship reserved for me.

> In the final scene of the dream, I was standing by an open round ship, wondering if I should leave... could I just abandon him? The feeling was very different. There was no panic, no worry, no sadness...

For a few days, I couldn't shake off that dream. It was so real, so...weird.

Finally, I decided to write him an email.

Looking back from where we are now, we would never, ever have even met let alone go on a spiritual journey together, without that whole series of synchronistic events.

REFERENCES

85.   [Photo]

Road to Jerome (Sedona, Arizona)

intheeternal.com/en/id/741

14

Buddha Buddy

"Who is holding who's hand,
promise to meet again in
this lifetime and next?"

— Author

Taipei, Taiwan
July 2012

"Hey, what are you going to say to your friends when they ask who I am?" Seann took a bottle of water, sat down in front of me, and handed me a few capsules of Spirulina.

I looked at him, my brain went totally blank, and even forgot to put the spirulina in my mouth.

"You could say we have known each other a long time, like thousands of years," he said laughing.

I didn't know how to respond. What should I tell people?

I divorced many years ago, and now I'm with a younger white guy. But we're not boyfriend and girlfriend...our relationship is much deeper than boyfriend and girlfriend. We are...let's say..."Buddha buddies."

Finally, I found a better way to describe us.

Asheville, North Carolina
September 2009

On the drive from Albuquerque to Sedona, right after I dropped him off at the airport; there was a clear scene of an evening breeze whipping up the early autumn leaves. Seann was standing next to a silver truck wearing dark sunglasses, looking up at the fading sunset in the sky....

When he invited me to visit him in North Carolina, I was not surprised, and booked my ticket without thinking much about it. After I got off the plane, I didn't see him at the gate, so I called him. He said he was waiting for me outside. I grabbed my luggage, walked out of the terminal and saw the same scene I had seen two months ago. He was standing next to a silver truck wearing dark sunglasses.

Dragging my luggage, I slowly walked toward him. He turned his head to look at me and noticed my luggage, including a very big suitcase. Concerns covered his face. He loaded all my stuff into his truck quietly.

I got into the truck, busy looking through my backpack and totally unaware of the awkward silence. When I happily pulled out the peaches I brought from California, and handed him the giant one with a paper towel, he suddenly burst out laughing.

"Is your huge suitcase full of food?"

"Yes! How do you know?"

"You startled me," he said, "I saw your big suitcase, and wasn't sure how long you planned to stay here."

"I used to travel a lot for work, and always travel light. My own personal stuff is just that little suitcase." I pointed to my heavy backpack and said proudly, "This is also full of food."

"You're afraid we will starve to death in the middle of nowhere?"

"I'm afraid I'll be starved to death by you in the middle of nowhere." I said laughing.

After eating the peaches Seann started talking, and talked the entire drive back to his cabin. Like a dutiful tour guide, he introduced every landscape in great detail. Like the valley where the comedian Steve Martin lives, the old radio telescope observatory, and so on.

Radio Telescope

"You've only been here a month, how do you know all of these details about the area?"

"I ask lots of questions...there is so much we don't know unless we ask. People have lived in these mountains for generations, and are usually eager to tell me what they know about the area."

The night in the mountains was very dark, the road was twisty and winding with almost no cars on the narrow lane. The lights of his truck seemed so dim, quickly dissipating into the immense blackness. We were turning and meandering, and continued climbing up.

"How did you find this place?" I asked him.

"Craigslist."

"Craigslist? You are very brave!"

"Yeah, there are some scammers on Craigslist, but it's only a small percentage. Besides, I believe as long as we have good intentions toward others, we will be fine."

"Are you a Buddhist?"

"I have read some books about Buddhism, and resonate with many of the teachings, but I don't put a label on what I believe."

After meeting, we have exchanged ideas about technology, quantum physics, climate issues, and more esoteric topics like earth changes and the end of world prophecy. From spiritual realization, evolution, to the meaning of life. However, religion had been left out of our never ending discussions.

"So, what about you?" He asked me. "Are you a Buddhist?"

"I believe in Jesus and Buddha's teaching, I'm just not interested in religious organizations established by people, even though they serve their purpose."

"That's great," he responded, with a hint of excitement. "Religion is a sensitive subject. I'm so glad you have a similar perspective as me, it's nice to speak freely."

Just then, he slowed down and turned into a small valley, a narrow road between trees. After a short drive, we emerged into total darkness again. Under the faint headlights, I noticed that we were on a dirt and gravel road.

"We are almost there." Seann turned and looked at me, "You are very brave. You came to this unfamiliar, in the middle of no where place, just because I invited you. You weren't afraid?"

"Why? You are here, what do I have to worry about?"

He stopped the truck, and shifted into park.

"Are we here?"

"Yes, we are here."

I got out of his truck and looked around. At the end of the driveway, deep in the woods, under the inviting moonlight, a fairy tale kind of old cabin was standing there quietly.

Whoa! I climbed up to the front porch and realized that we were above the clouds. Sparkling stars filled the sky, hanging so low, almost like I could touch them with my hands. The flowing mist reflecting moonlight on treetops, smothering the forest and the cabin...

"Stars hanging down over the wide open fields,
Emanating moonlights flowing like an enormous river."

It was so beautiful, I could hardly breathe.

"Ah!..." A white shadowy figure dashed to my side, I was frightened and jumped away instinctively.

"Shiva!" Seann ran over quickly, with one hand holding my shaking body and another hand caressing the dog. "It's surprising that she didn't bark at you. I think she likes you!"

"Little kids and animals, they all like me." I responded with confidence, and walked over to Shiva and reached out with my hand, "Come, let's shake hands!"

Shiva looked at me confused.

"Shiva didn't go to doggie school?"

"She can sit and catch, and in Austin she swam in the creek behind the cabin almost everyday. She knows the important stuff, but yeah, she still has some things to learn. She is only one, so there is still time."

I smiled at Seann and continued to play with Shiva.

"Poor Shiva, just like Diamond, doggy school deprived!" I was joking and rubbing her belly when Seann's voice appeared behind me.

"Do you have dog?"

"Yes, two! A golden retriever and a Siberian husky."

"No wonder Shiva is so friendly with you." Seann was standing by the doorway, "Come on in, I'll show you the house."

I stood up, walking toward Seann. Shiva sprinted over and squeezed in between me and Seann.

"Shiva. She is a friend, no need to worry. Go, play with your toys." Seann petted Shiva, coaxing her softly, trying to get her to relax.

Since I've known him, we had many intellectual discussions, but that was the first time I saw the sensitive side of him. I was somehow deeply moved.

"Shiva is very protective, she never allows anyone to get close to me, even my Dad." Seann with his typical gentlemen like smile, pointed to the room behind the living room, "that's the guest room. I moved all of your luggage in there already."

"Thank you!"

"Like I mentioned, my brother left this afternoon, and I did laundry. So, sheets, blanket, comforter, everything is fresh." He looked at me apologetically, "Laundry took too long, that's why I was late. When you called me, I was just driving in to the airport. Sorry that I didn't make it to the gate."

"That's ok, it doesn't matter." I remember he told me over the phone that his brother came to visit. "How did he like it here?"

"He loved it. If I stay for a while, he would like to come again and stay longer next time."

As he was speaking, he led me up an iron spiral staircase to the second floor. "That is the master bedroom, over there is my office area."

I walked to the front of the bookcases, naturally.

"You're like me, always looking at books, eh?" He asked.

"Yeah, I grew up poor, we hardly had much material stuff, but my parents never restricted me from buying books. Books were an important part of my childhood. When most of my friends would go shopping, I would go to book fair or art gallery."

"That's interesting..." He smiled, then walked to his desk and sat down, turning the chair to look at me before continuing. "In school I didn't socialize much. Looking back it was actually a good thing, because I spent a lot of time in the library. Later in life I spent a lot of time at bookstores, and every time I found a good book, I would buy several copies and give it to people."

"Really? I do that too."

I turned to look at the books, but was not impressed.

"Those are my landlord's." Seann seemed to hear what I was thinking.

I am pretty careful with the books I read, too many of them are full of nonsense. Confucius's successor Mencius famously said, "If you believe everything written in every book, it's better that you just throw away all the books." There is also an old Chinese saying, a teacher will go to the 19th level of hell if he mislead his students. I was thinking about that, but kept silent. After all, we were still just getting to know each other.

Then I noticed several of the *Conversations with God*[88] books, and asked, "Have you read those?"

"I read the first one, yeah. I also bought his new one, *When Everything Changes, Change Everything*[89], and had planned to read it while here. How about you?"

"I only read *The New Revelations*[90]. That was really good. After reading that book I signed up to his Daily Inspirations, which is pretty amazing."

At that moment, I realized my harsh judgment of the books on the bookshelves, and wanted to be more appreciative. "What do you think about the first Conversations with God book?"

"Well, my mom's parents were Catholic, and we went to a Christian church every Sunday when I was growing up, so the basic concepts are familiar. But, seeing someone put religious teachings into plain language was very refreshing, and in my opinion long overdue. God didn't stop speaking thousands of years ago, despite what some people would like us to believe."

He became animated, sitting up in his chair, and continued, "There have been a lot of inspired writings over the millennia, and the people who wrote the texts that were included in the Bible probably had a very similar experience." He turned, pointing to *A Course in Miracles*[91], which was sitting next to his keyboard, "And it's the same with this book too."

"Is that one yours?"

"Yeah. Are you familiar with it?"

"Kind of."

"What do you think about it?"

"I understand, in theory, I think. But it's Gary Renard's books that helped me to grasp the teachings."

"Yeah, *Disappearance of the Universe*[92] is pretty entertaining."

I noticed a faint fatigue in his eyes.

"Anyway, it's late," he said, acknowledging my concerned look. "It's been a long day for both of us, we can talk more in the morning."

"Ya, we have 10 more days." I walked towards the stairs and said jokingly, "It looks like there's not much we can do but talk on this mountain top."

REFERENCES

86. [Photo]

Buddha Buddies (Hsi Lai Temple, California)

intheeternal.com/en/id/820

87. [Photo]

PARI Radio Telescope (Pisgah National Forest)

intheeternal.com/en/id/480

88. [Book]

Walsch, N. D. (1998) Conversations with God

intheeternal.com/en/id/806

89.
[Book]
Walsch, N. D. (2009) *When Everything Changes, Change Everything*
intheeternal.com/en/id/788

90.
[Book]
Walsch, N. D. (2008) *The New Revelations*
intheeternal.com/en/id/804

91.
[Book]
Schucman, H. (1976) *A Course in Miracles*
intheeternal.com/en/id/525

92.
[Book]
Renard, G. (2002) *Disappearance of the Universe*
intheeternal.com/en/id/810

15

Awakening

"Life was never meant to be a struggle,
just a gentle progression from one
point to another, much like walking
through a valley on a sunny day."

— Stuart Wilde

Pisgah National Forest, North Carolina
September 2009

The sunlight shined through the colored glass bottles plastered into the log cabin wall, onto my closed eyes. I woke up from my dream, a little puzzled about where I was.

There was a scent of fallen leaves in the cool air. I sat up, and slowly came back to reality. It seemed like the whole space was still and time had stopped. The only thing seemed real was the five faces in my dream, one morphing into another...

Materialized from realizations,
Accompanied by inspirations,
Rising out of dreams...

I don't know why those lines emerged in my mind.

"Where will this mysterious path take me?" I asked silently, not expecting to find answer.

I got out of bed, put on a sweater, and stepped into the living room. Seann was on the porch outside, smoking and talking on the phone. Shiva, his yellow Labrador, saw me from the window and quickly ran in through the doggie door. She came up to me wagging her tail, dropped the ball in her mouth down in front of me.

As I was rubbing Shiva's belly, Seann opened the door and walked in.

"Good morning! Did you sleep well?"

"Yes."

Before I could say another word, the phone rang again.

"Sorry, I have to take this call." He looked at me with apologetic eyes.

"No problem, work is important." I said to him, trying to ease his discomfort.

Seann went back out to the porch, and Shiva followed him. As he talked on the phone, he was throwing ball with Shiva. They looked happy playing together.

The cabin was on a hilltop encircled by national forest, with views of the surrounding mountains and the valley below. No sounds of cars in the distance, no sight of other houses, just green forest as far as I could see.

After his call he came back in to the kitchen and started grinding coffee beans. "Sorry, I was not expecting calls this morning."

Shiva hoped up on the couch, ready for a nap.

"Actually, I came here to get away from all of that," he said, pouring hot water over the coffee. "I referred my clients to other people before leaving Austin, and the guy I was just talking to was one of them."

"Was it hard leaving your life in Austin? Do you miss it?"

"Not at all, no. I tried it a few years ago, it just didn't work out." He looked at me, "Would you like honey in your coffee?"

"Sure, but just a little."

North Carolina - Shiva

He washed a couple of coffee cups, and poured our coffee, saying very deliberately, "Years ago I spoke with Hans King[79] for the first time. He is a medium."

He brought our coffee to the dining table and sat down.

"So, when Hans was young people noticed he could get information from the spirit world. Later he went to the College of Psychic Studies[95] in England. It's like a Harry Potter school, where they train people who are naturally gifted."

I looked at my coffee, contemplating if I should tell him... "My father told me not to visit psychics. He said the more you have your fortune told, the worse it would get."

He nodded but continued the topic anyway. "Have you heard of Edgar Cayce"[96]?

"Of course."

"Sometimes the information we get, like with Cayce, we can see our life from a higher perspective. Conscious beings in the higher dimensional realms have access to the Book of Life, or the Akashic Records. And some people can get information from those beings, and bring it to us here, in this limited material reality that appears to be all there is." He looked at Shiva napping on the couch. "That is what Hans did, but instead of going into a trance like Cayce, he communicated with his guides consciously."

"What did he tell you?" I asked curiously, before realizing it was a very personal question.

"He said a lot, but one thing that stuck out...he said I was going to write a book. He also said to start taking notes, and suggested recording my thoughts and observations." He took another sip of coffee. "I have studied metaphysical subjects since my teen years, and often attempted to put what I had learned into terms that people could understand, so it kind of made sense. Anyway, I always felt that being an electronics guy was not my purpose in life." He said, staring out the window, deep in thought.

"So..." After a few moments, he started, then paused, with some hesitation. "About your email..."

After I sent him an email explaining what happened to me on the way back to California, we had only talked on the phone briefly. The reason he invited me to North Carolina, was so we could spend some time together, and I could tell him what I knew about that lifetime.

He broke the silence after we both got quiet for a moment. "I have been reading a couple of books by Princess Derling[97], have you heard of her?"

"Sounds familiar."

"She spent two years at the Forbidden City after Pearl died. Reading some of the stories..." he paused, and I noticed he was getting teary-eyed. "There is a lot of emotion around that life, but, I don't really understand, because I don't know the history. In a way, I think it would be easier to not know, then I could just write my silly, feel good metaphysical book."

"I didn't want to talk about it when I called you two weeks ago, there is too much sadness." I said, hesitantly. "When I was in Taiwan last month, I bought some books about that period. It was raining outside, so the noise covered the sound of my sadness. I couldn't stop crying."

After a few deep breaths I continued, "There is still a lot of hurt and sadness, and strong feelings of injustice from that life, which is why I haven't wanted to look at it."

"Right, I agree. So today, we won't talk about it. You will be here for a while," he said, pointing at the bowl of Asian pears on the table, "We have to eat all of that fruit before you go."

He got up from his chair, waking Shiva from her nap. "Maybe we could go for a drive today, there are some really nice waterfalls nearby."

"Yeah, that sounds perfect."

"What do you think Shiva, do you want to go for a ride?"

Shiva hopped off the couch and ran to the door, tail wagging...

North Carolina - Looking Glass

The rest of my time in North Carolina was spent exploring the mountains, waterfalls, and of course having lots of long conversations.

One morning we were talking about the book he was writing, when he asked if I wanted to see it.

"This binder has notes I have been taking these last few years, and an outline. I haven't finalized the Chapter titles, but the framework is mostly in place."

I took the binder and started reading what he had written. Some of his handwriting was hard to read, so I walked over to the window where the light was brighter.

"Sorry for my messy writing." he said apologetically.

"It's not that bad. At my age, almost all of my friends are wearing glasses, maybe I should get reading glasses too, haha." I laughed but quickly went back to reading...

"I'll take Shiva out for a walk, happy reading..."

Shiva ran thru the doggie door and happily greeted me, then went to the couch for a nap. Seann opened the door, walked in, and saw me still reading his folder.

"What do you think? Should I quit now and go back to being an electronics guy?" he said with a sarcastic tone, "I am not a writer, so you won't hurt my feelings."

"I didn't get too far but really like it."

His eyes lit up, "which part?"

"Your experience in the Vancouver hotel, where you talk about that bad dream. You can't shine darkness...how does that go?"

"It came to me after a meditation, but that was two years ago. Here, it's in this journal..." he said, flipping thru a black notebook he took off the shelf.

"There is nothing to fear, ever, anyone. Evil is ignorance, the
absence of understanding. There is light and the absence of
light in varying degrees. It's not a matter of evil overcoming
good, for that is impossible as it can't exist when in the presence
of understanding. There is no power in darkness, only absence
of light, which causes misunderstanding. Just as it is impossible
to shine darkness into the light, it is impossible for ignorance
to overcome understanding, for once understanding is
present, ignorance cannot remain. Fear not, now that
this understanding is present, ignorance has no power,
therefore evil cannot exist in the presence of your light."

"Yeah, that! That is really interesting and profound!"

"Anything else?"

"The meeting by the fireside…"

"Is that too weird, or did it make sense?"

"Do you mean all of our past life personalities still co-exist with our current self in a different dimension? I think it makes sense, and it's kind of a new angle."

"Well, my impression was that if each of our previous incarnations are projections from our higher self, then maybe we can all gather around a fire and share stories from our life experiences. And *maybe* some of our spirit guides are really us, or other aspects of our own soul. That is what I was trying to say."

"That could be true…"

"Maybe so. I am learning to trust these insights more."

I hesitated for a minute, "I don't understand why you gave up everything to come here and write. Couldn't you do that in Austin? Why come here?"

"I wasn't happy, is the short answer."

"And what is the longer answer?"

"So, in 2005 when Hans said that I was going to write a book, I started working on an outline. By 2007 I had a lot of notes, but was very busy juggling a lot of projects, and didn't have time to write.

Then a lot of little synchronicities started happening, and I interpreted that as a sign it was time to start winding down my business to focus full-time on writing. There was a feeling something was missing, but intuitively it seemed that if I kept moving forward, it would all come together and make sense."

"What do you think was missing?"

"Meeting you, and learning about the past. I have read all kinds of books, had tarot card readings, talked with astrologers, psychics and mediums, took lots of self-improvement workshops, you name it. A lot of good came from all of it, and I learned a lot, but there was some underlying unhappiness that didn't make sense until we met and you told me about 100 years ago. Now, after reading the Derling books, it makes sense."

"What makes sense?"

"In Albuquerque I told you about watching The Last Emperor movie many times, and the feeling that maybe I had lived there before. But..." he hesitated, then continued. "There is something else. It sounds ridiculous, but for many years, I was actually afraid of being poisoned. Anytime there was leftover food in the refrigerator, I wouldn't eat it. It was the same thing with wine. Each time I would think of eating or drinking something that was already open, that completely irrational fear would come up, and it usually ended up in the trash."

"How long...when did that start?"

"Probably about 4 years ago, after moving to Austin. But, after reading about Guangxu being poisoned, that totally irrational fear made sense. The funny thing is, these last few weeks I haven't worried about food being poisoned. A few times I hesitated out of habit, but was able to brush it off easily, because now it's clear where that comes from. It's from the past."

I laughed, "That's good, because there isn't much to eat around here."

He smiled and nodded his head, then looked at me as if he remembered something. "Have you heard of Brian Weiss?"

"Yea." I nodded.

"One of his stories about people carrying unconscious memories of past life trauma into their present life, was about a man who was afraid of heights. He had a past life regression and remembered falling off a cliff in a previous lifetime, and after that, he lost his fear of heights. Interesting, eh?"

"Yeah, I have heard a few stories like that too."

"A couple of other things make more sense too, after reflecting on all of this these last few weeks."

"Like what?"

"Well, I have worked for a lot of rich and famous people in my career, but I wasn't intimidated by any of them. I think that once we live lifetimes as significant people, we probably aren't as impressed or intimidated by people who are playing those roles in this life, because we have been in similar circumstances before. If anything, we probably have more empathy and understanding of the situation they are in. And, that also explains why I never chased after money or power. I actually walked away from a lot of opportunities over the years, because I wasn't willing to sacrifice my independence. Freedom was always the most important thing to me."

"Me too." I thought but remained silent so not to interfere with his story.

"Anyway, what I am saying is that we carry the essence of who we are as a soul with us from life to life, and the non-verbal communication between people conveys some of that, even if we aren't consciously aware of it."

"So about the other thing you mentioned, what makes more sense now?"

"Yeah, so I read that Guangxu liked to take apart clocks, and that he had electricity and telegraph service installed in some parts of the Forbidden City. Did you know that?"

"No, I didn't know about that."

"Well, I took apart clocks and radios when I was a kid too. And, I also designed lighting and telephone systems. When I read that it made sense, those interests carried over to this lifetime. This whole reincarnation thing is very interesting. I have been doing a lot of research this last week, and ordered a couple of reference books by Sylvia Cranson[98]. It looks like I will have to add a chapter about reincarnation, now that this has come up."

Reincarnation

Another morning while having coffee Seann asked, "You never told me about your second recurring dream." One night, after dinner, Seann asked, "In Albuquerque at the IHOP you mentioned two dreams, but you only told me the first one."

"Yeah, it was too much to talk about then…"

"Do you want to tell me now?"

"The first dream, just like what I told you before, I didn't really understand until I went to the Forbidden City. In the other dream, I was just sinking. There were bricks on the side, I could see the bricks, and I was sinking down and down...in slow motion."

His eyes widened, "That is what happened to Pearl, I read about that in Derling's books. Your dream was her drowning in the well."

I did not respond, just trying to stay calm.

Suddenly, it looked like he remembered something. "And that is probably what my dream was about, in Albuquerque. It wasn't a box someone was drowning in, it was a well."

We both sat in silence for quite a few moments, letting the story sink in.

"I would always wake up from that dream sweating. I didn't understand... Of course, I knew the story...all Chinese know that story." In the Forbidden City, there still has the well where Pearl drowned being carefully preserved as one of the popular tourist spots.

He seemed engulfed by the sadness, so I tried to bring up a happier topic. "I met my sister from that lifetime."

"Jin Fei[99]?" He asked in surprise.

"Yeah. She was much more aware than me. Even back then, she was able to stay out of all the power struggles and avoid controversy. She told me she remembered who she was in that life."

He just sat there, looking at me. Even though I could tell he had many questions, I continued...

"Before Jin Fei died, while she was Dowager Imperial Consort for Puyi[100], she chose one of the Manchurian royal families to give the arts she collected all those years. Then, she reincarnated into that family so she could have them in this life again."

"She told you that?" He asked, surprised again.

"That is what she told me."

"How did you meet her?"

"Someone told her about Jennifer, my Qigong teacher, so she flew to LA to meet with her. That is how we met. She stayed for a few days so we were hanging out quite a lot in those days. When she was leaving town I drove her to the airport...it was chilly so I gave her my jacket to keep her warm. She asked if I needed anything, and I told her no. Later she sent some expensive Chanel[47] cosmetics to me, and told me to take good care of myself. I knew what she told me was true, I trust her."

"So she recognized you? She knew who you were?"

"Yeah. After that meeting she told Jennifer I was Pearl, but I didn't want to believe it. I was stubborn."

"When was that?"

"In the mid 1990's"

"Wow, so you have known since then?" He stared out the window, reflecting on the story. I hadn't really thought much about it in a long time, then I remembered something that made me laugh.

"What is so funny?"

"One day, I was having a heated discussion with Thomas about some current event, and Jennifer said, shaking her head, 'If you weren't so opinionated, maybe you wouldn't have been thrown into the well!'"

"Yeah, we haven't known each other long, but I can see you are very opinionated." He said jokingly. "But, that is also why I like you..."

One day I asked why he chose this place.

"For a long time I have wanted to have a place in the country, maybe a small farm. I needed someplace quiet to write, and this place seemed like a good opportunity to see what it was like living remotely."

"Really?" I asked excitedly, "I always wanted a farm too. When I was young, I loved being in nature, and missed it when we moved to Taipei. Why do you want a farm?"

"Have you heard of the movie Koyaanisqatsi[101]"?

I shook my head, "No."

"Well, that movie is the reason why. It's a Hopi word that means 'life out of balance'. That movie, for me, was important because it captured the essence of what I had felt about our modern world. We have lost touch with what is important, and instead spend our time rushing around doing things, but aren't conscious of where it is all leading. Anyway, I will buy you a copy of the DVD, it's definitely worth watching."

"Okay, sure. It sounds interesting."

"My grandparents have a place in the country, I loved visiting them when I was younger. They had about 50 cows, a huge garden and a pond. I would fish in the pond, and watch the hummingbirds and the ducks at the feeders my grandmother set out for them, it was so peaceful. And besides, I am not a big fan of cities. In my early 20's I spent 3 years commuting to downtown Houston everyday for work." He said, laughing. "I swore when I was done with that job, I would never wear a tie again."

"Have you?" I asked, curious.

"Nope. I haven't worn a tie since 1994." He said, proudly.

"While working downtown, I found out about Intentional Communities[102]. They are places where people go to live and work, a lot of them are farms, and that caught my interest. After some visits to the Houston Public Library to browse the directory, and sending out a few letters, I got a few responses and an invitation to participate in a work exchange program."

"What kind of work?"

"Things like picking weeds out of the garden, watering trees, that kind of thing. I also learned to make carob brownies, and very tasty pesto using the basil I picked from the garden. It was a place in Arizona called Reevis Mountain School of Self Reliance[103].

I spent four months there, mostly helping in the garden, feeding the chickens and cleaning up the chicken coop. I will never forget the smell of chicken poop."

Feeding Chickens (1994)

He made a disgusted face. I had never seen him so animated and burst out laughing.

"Was that why you left?"

"No, I decided that one day I would have my own place, and if I stayed too long, that probably would not happen. It was a lot of hard work, especially for a city kid, but I never seen so many stars at night. And there was an old abandoned Native American village nearby that I liked hiking to, just to experience the silence. There was also a creek flowing thru the property that was very refreshing after an afternoon in the garden.

It was nice being someplace with no TV, no telephone, spring fed water, and food that I picked from the garden. That experience changed the way I look at life, and makes our modern world seem chaotic by comparison. Koyaanisqatsi."

Two weeks flew by swiftly.... what I didn't know was my life had taken an unexpected turn, one that eventually changed everything...

Arizona (1994)

REFERENCES

93. [Photo]

Morning Mist (Pisgah National Forest)

intheeternal.com/en/id/479

94.
[Photo]
Shiva on Couch (Pisgah National Forest)
intheeternal.com/en/id/481

79.
[Note]
Hans Christian King : About
intheeternal.com/en/id/528

95.
[Link]
College of Psychic Studies
intheeternal.com/en/id/790

96.
[Link]
Edgar Cayce : About
intheeternal.com/en/id/791

97.
[Link]
Princess Derling : Wikipedia page
intheeternal.com/en/id/805

98.
[Book]
Cranston, S. (1998) *Reincarnation : The Phoenix Fire Mystery*
intheeternal.com/en/id/602

99.
[Note]
Jin Fei : Imperial Noble Consort Wenjing
intheeternal.com/en/id/529

100. [Note]

Puyi : The Last Emperor

intheeternal.com/en/id/530

47. [Note]

Chanel – Reincarnation Video

intheeternal.com/en/id/526

101. [Link]

Koyaanisqatsi : Movie

intheeternal.com/en/id/792

102. [Link]

Intentional Communities

intheeternal.com/en/id/793

103. [Link]

Reevis Mountain School : website

intheeternal.com/en/id/794

104. [Photo]

Feeding Chickens (Maricopa County, Arizona)

intheeternal.com/en/id/430

105. [Photo]

Arizona Desert (Maricopa County, Arizona)

intheeternal.com/en/id/429

16

Turning Point

"Sorrow prepares you for joy. It violently
sweeps everything out of your house, so
that new joy can find space to enter. It
shakes the yellow leaves from the bough of
your heart, so that fresh, green leaves
can grow in their place. It pulls up the
rotten roots, so that new roots hidden
beneath have room to grow. Whatever
sorrow shakes from your heart, far
better things will take their place."

— Rumi

Pisgah National Forest, North Carolina
November 2009

Five weeks later, I came back to the cabin to help Seann pack and
move. The first visit helped me clear some of the sadness I had
been carrying my whole life, and he said the same thing happened
for him. Since I had a guest house that wasn't being used, I invited
him to work on his book in LA so he didn't have to spend winter
alone in the mountains.

On the drive to Texas, in the mountains of South Carolina, Seann
was quietly reflecting on things, and I knew he was about to say
something important. He always looks so serious when he is deep

in thought, and I had learned to let him speak when he was ready, rather than asking what he was thinking.

He was driving his truck towing a U-Haul trailer, and Shiva was uncomfortable with the bumpy ride, quietly slumped in the back seat trying to sleep. The late afternoon sun casting a layer of golden hue over the autumn colors of the trees. I was busy looking around, admiring the beauty of the Appalachian Mountains.

After awhile he started explaining what he had been thinking, "I thought I could help people by writing what I had learned from my spiritual experience over the years. That's why I came to these mountains..."

"And that's how I could have the opportunity to come!" I said jokingly.

"Yeah, true. But now, it seems I needed to learn about the past. Without understanding reincarnation, anything I would have written about my spiritual journey would not have been complete. So, thanks for inviting me to LA. I am not a fan of big cities, but I would rather spend the winter in Los Angeles than alone in the mountains."

I kept silent and turned back to pet Shiva. She wagged her tail, looked up at Seann and me briefly, then laid back down.

To ease the silent tension, I reached into the bag for a cookie, "Are you hungry?"

"A little." He took the cookie, hesitated, then gave it back to me, "Actually, I'd like some tea, if you don't mind."

I opened the thermos and handed it to him.

He thanked me. After a few sips he asked, "Are you tired?"

"No."

He smiled slightly, "I want to get out of the mountains before it gets dark, so we won't stop, is that okay?"

"I'm not driving, as long as you're not tired, I'm fine."

That night, we drove through outskirts of Atlanta and headed into Alabama before stopping at a hotel.

North Carolina - Leaving the Mountains

The next day we were talking while driving through Louisiana. He asked why I was still living with my ex-husband. "Isn't that awkward?"

"I did it for the kids. For a while I had my own house nearby, and they would come stay with me when I wasn't out of town for work."

"That does sound like quite a hassle for them. Moving back and forth."

"Yeah, so, after my parents passed away, we decided to build a bigger house on property that we owned nearby. I was able to design it the way I wanted, including the guest house where you will be staying. It was a lot of work for me managing the construction, but living together was easier for everyone. I have my own room, and now that the kids are in college, I have the whole place to myself most of the time."

"So, he knows I am coming?"

"No, but it won't bother him. He travels out of town a lot and the guest house is completely separate from the main house."

"Sounds like he is a decent person why did you..." he hesitated...

"Divorce him?" It's a sensitive subject, so I opened the conversation. "He is very smart, and has a big heart, that's why I married him. But, I wasn't happy, and was getting pretty sick."

"I remember you mentioned that's why you started practicing QiGong."

"Yeah. Practicing QiGong restored my health, and I was able to rebuild my career. For me, being independent is very important."

"Yeah, I can see that. You are too opinionated to not be independent." He tried not to laugh and I bursted out laughing.

"You know John Denver right?"

"You're talking about the singer?"

"Yeah. His wife married him before he was successful and divorced him even though he was rich and famous. She went back to school and got a Masters degree in Psychology so she could help people. That's the kind of woman I admire."

He looked at me a little confused.

"Asian women are usually more submissive. When things are not working well, not many would initiate a divorce." I paused and reflected on the past, "We, Dr. Chen and I, had different values, perspectives, and goals for life."

"Do you regret it?"

"Yes and no. I love my daughters, they are the most important people in my life. I think the divorce did have some negative impact, but it also had some positive effects too."

"So, if you focus on the positive, do you think it was a good decision?"

"I think so, yeah. I was able to develop my own career, and spend more time with my daughters."

— 🀄 —

The day after, we arrived in Houston. There was still time before my flight back to LA, so we went to an IHOP for pancakes and coffee.

"What are you going to do, stay with your parents?" I asked.

"They have some property north of Houston, so that is my next stop. I left some furniture and things in storage there that I need to sell or donate. Actually, I will be doing the same with a lot of the stuff in the trailer too. Most of what I brought to North Carolina was never unpacked. One thing is for sure, I won't be bringing a U-Haul to California."

"That's a good idea, I should do that too. Our garage is so full of stuff that we can't park any cars inside."

He nodded, then looked around the restaurant, lost in thought.

"It's funny... In a way, spending so much time and energy storing, maintaining and hauling our stuff around, is similar to carrying around our karma. Every time I give away, donate or recycle stuff that isn't needed, I feel lighter, more free. And, it's the same with our unprocessed mental or emotional stuff, we feel better when we let it go. The trick is to not be attached to something just because it was once significant, if it is no longer needed."

I smiled, letting him finish his thoughts.

"There is a saying, 'The more stuff you own, the more it owns you.' It's true, but it also applies to our karma. A lot of us hold onto ideas of who we think we are, and the stories we tell ourselves about our lives. These last few weeks I have started to let that go, and now I feel more free. It's an interesting thing. Less really is more."

After the late lunch, we made the short drive to the airport terminal in silence. It was difficult to park the truck towing a U-Haul trailer, so we drove to the departure gate. After he managed to squeeze his way thru the traffic to the curb, I jumped out, said goodbye to him and Shiva quickly, promised to see them in Los Angeles in about a month.

After I entered the airport lobby, I turned and watched through the window. He seemed pretty calm, navigating his truck and trailer through the overcrowded airport traffic, slowly moving away. While waiting for the plane, a mild anxiety expanded into a faint panic. It felt like I was treading on a thin ice, in danger of falling through at any moment.

Los Angeles, California
November 2009

With a heavy heart, I flew back to Los Angeles. I told my ex-husband, Dr. Chen, that I had invited Seann to come and stay with us.

"Can you trust this guy? How well do you know him?" He asked.

"I know the names and have information about his family, friends, even some of his clients; I also have his mom's phone number, is that enough?"

"He's a weird guy." After a pause, he said, "I know you like to help people, but do you know what he is really thinking? Why is he coming here?"

"He is the most sincere, kind and good-hearted person I have ever met. And I just wanted to give him a quiet and stable environment so he can focus on writing." I replied.

"Oh! He's a writer?" He asked surprisingly.

"No, he's an engineer."

"In what field?"

"Home automation, computers, and networks."

"What kind of book is he writing?"

"It's about spirituality." I responded in an irritated tone.

"Can he make money with writing that kind of book?"

"How do I know?"

"No one wants to read that kind of book, it's a waste of time! Why doesn't he just go back to his job as an engineer and make more money?" He said, being the pragmatic engineer he has always been.

He is intelligent and creative, a very talented aerospace engineer, but unfortunately, like many people, he thinks money is the most important indicator of one's accomplishment in life. Even though I know he is a nice person, kind and giving, our different world view and value system have been difficult to reconcile.

I didn't want to discuss with him any more, so I found an excuse and went to my room.

Although Dr. Chen did not look for trouble, I was no longer so sure about the up coming situation. My two daughters were traveling around the world with Semester at Sea, currently on the way from Shanghai to Japan. Tomorrow, I need to deposit money into their account.

Also, I need to find someone to clean the guest house. And we should finally install an awning over the second floor balcony...

That night, I must have fallen asleep with a frown on my face. A shadow had loomed on the horizon. What kind of trouble had I gotten myself into?

REFERENCES

106. [Photo]
Fall Trees (Pisgah National Forest)
intheeternal.com/en/id/828

107. [Photo]
Leaving the Mountains (Pisgah National Forest)
intheeternal.com/en/id/600

17

Gods Gifts

*"Once we turn that corner and believe in
the spiritual dimension of life, we
can then go much deeper into the
precise way spirituality actually works."*

— James Redfield

Los Angeles, California
December 2009

In mid-December, my two daughters were returning from their Semster at Sea program, and some of their friends were preparing for the "Welcome Home" party. We lived in a small 'bedroom' community, where everyone knows everyone and their siblings. These kids grew up together, and had been hanging out at our house ever since we finished building it.

When I was pregnant with our first daughter, Bo-Bo is her nickname, I endured morning sickness until almost all the way till I gave birth. When I was pregnant with Xiang-Xiang, I was sick for about six months.

After Xiang-Xiang was born, I was still sick physically and stressed out trying to build a different career so I could have more flexible time to take care of my daughters. One day, I went to St. John's church and knelt down asked for help.

Out of nowhere, Yuan-Yuan appeared.

After I was pregnant with our youngest, Yuan-Yuan, for four months, my secretary saw I was always tired and asked me if I were pregnant. I said with no hesitation, "That's not possible, I've had two children, how could I not know if I'm pregnant?"

During my first pregnancy, Dr. Chen said jokingly, "We'd better not have a daughter who looks like me but has your temperament, then we're screwed." When Yuan-Yuan came, his 'fear' finally materialized. But, contrary to his perception, Yuan-Yuan was super popular and I believe it was her personality and the energy she brought with her that attracted all the attention.

Teachers and parents at our local Chinese school called her "Wan ren mi (A heartthrob with ten thousand fans)."' I called her my "Little Buddha." But she described herself as my "year-round entertainment." Ever since she could write, she would write love letters to me, to her father, to her teachers, and to her tennis coach...

One time I took a group of kids to a bowling alley, and Tammy came to tell me after a few games, "AuYi, Yuan-Yuan is beating all of us."

"Really?"

"Yea! Do you want to see how she did it?"

"Sure!" I followed Tammy to the lanes where they were playing.

Yuan-Yuan was barely six years old, kind of small for her age, and didn't talk much. But many of the older kids, like Tammy, loved her dearly.

"Yuan-Yuan, do you want to show your mom how you play?" Tammy said to her. She gave me a broad smile then walked to the balls, used both hands to hold a bowling ball like it was a watermelon, walked to the lane, dropped the ball then ran fast to me. I grabbed her, holding her up to watch that ball, and somehow it found it's way down the center and knocked over all the pins. "Strike!!!" Flashed on the video screen on top of the lane.

Occasionally, I would run into her old teachers or some parents from Chinese school at the supermarket, they always asked me, "How old is Yuan-Yuan now? She's still so cute huh!"

Well known medium James Von Praagh pointed out that people respond not so much to our look but our presence, and Yuan-Yuan is just the living proof for that concept.

There is a saying that God's gifts come in packages of different sizes and shapes. My three daughters are truly evidence of that. I could never understand, "Life is much more magical than logical," before my daughters showed up in my life.

After dinner, I was a little woozy from the wine so I went upstairs early. I saw a call from Seann on my cell phone and slapped my head, I almost forgot about him. Just when I was contemplating if I should call him back, the phone rang.

"Hello!"

"Hey, I was just going to leave you a message. Did your daughters make it back?"

"Yeah, everything's fine. How about you?"

"I'm good. So, my mother decided to drive with me to San Diego. She wants to spend Christmas with my brother and his kids. After I go to LA, she'll fly back to Houston."

"That's good. You're ..... which day do you think you'll arrive?"

"We are leaving tomorrow, so probably just before Christmas Eve."

Two days before Christmas, Bo-Bo returned home from New York, and a group of friends and acquaintances began to show up at the house. That afternoon, Seann arrived too. He was overwhelmed by all of the activities at my house. Cars were parked everywhere, even along the street below (my house is built on a hill), and young men and women of all races and ages were coming and going...

Over the years, being a mother and teacher, I have treated my daughters' friends as if they were my own children, at least the best I could. With our large house, my open-minded attitude, Dr. Chen's busy schedule and frequent business trips out of town, our home had become a gathering place for these kids.

But since Yuan-Yuan went off to college, this big empty nest was usually occupied by just me and my two dogs. As long as I didn't have to go to Santa Barbara to take care things for them, I was happy to stay home and relax.

Life is really unpredictable and full of surprises. As a child, I hated school and did not like to study, but now I would stay up all night reading or watching videos about quantum physics, spirituality, and all kinds of documentary or interviews, sometimes even forgetting to eat.

Over the years, the more I searched, the more confused I became. I wanted to find the real answers to my questions about life. Later I realized it's an impossible task, we cannot understand the infinite universe in the limited time or perception we have.

In my heart, perhaps I was really longing to understand what Henry Ford, the founder of Ford motor company, said in a 1938 interview with Hearst Newspapers:

"I adopted the theory of Reincarnation when I was 26.... Work is futile if we cannot utilize the experience we collect in one life to the next. When I discovered Reincarnation it was as if I had found a universal plan.... Time is no longer limited. I was no longer a slave to the hands of the clock.... Genius is experience. Some seem to think that it is a gift or talent, but it is the fruit of long experience in many lives. Some are older souls than others, and so they know more... The discovery of Reincarnation put my mind at ease. I would like to communicate to others the calmness that this long view of life gives to me."

Los Angeles, California
December 2009

I showed Seann around the guest house and introduced him to my two dogs. Dean and Diamond loved him right away. The year he was in Los Angeles, was the healthiest and happiest year for those two dogs. He gave them a lot of attention, partly because he decided to not bring Shiva to LA.

He knew there would be some instability over the coming years, which would not be good for a young dog. Coincidentally, at the same time his friend was looking for a Labrador for his property, and loved Shiva. He struggled with the decision, but since they were looking for a Labrador anyway, he asked if they would be interested in adopting Shiva.

That night, the winter air was as cool as spring water. We stood in front of the guest house, talking, as my daughters friends were gathering in the dance room above us. On the drive to my house from San Diego, he had decided that coming to Los Angeles for Christmas was not a good decision. His mom and brother were in San Diego, and my kids were going to be home for Christmas. He thought it made more sense for him to spend Christmas with his family, and come back later.

Under the moonlight, his face was half covered
by the shadow. Suddenly, it was like I had
been hit by a lighting. This scene ...... like
Déjà vu... seemed like, I've seen it before!

It was the same moonlight, same cool air, and
we were separated by a window. I rested
my head on the window sill and listened to him
talk hopefully about his plans for the future,
our future... all those unrealized dreams...

That young girl, was that me? Curled
up in a corner, in despair, crying...

"Do you understand what I mean?" He was confused by my unresponsiveness, and I didn't tell him what I saw. He said again, a little more insistently, "It's Christmas time. You should focus on your family and I should go back to San Diego to be with my family."

"You're always like this, so indecisive." I bursted out suddenly.

He froze for a moment, then said with a puzzled look. "Why do you say that?"

"Nothing," I said, turning away and wiping the tears from my eyes. "I'll tell the kids to move their cars."

"No need, I can back around them."

I turned on the lights for the guest house parking area and walked down with him to his truck.

He skillfully backed up his truck, going around the car parked behind him without hitting the retaining curb on the other side, with what looked like a fraction of a centimeter to spare on either side. A few kids, leaning over the balcony above the drive way, watched the scene with amazement.

As he was about to drive out of the gate, I walked toward his truck waving goodbye. He rolled down the window and said with a smile, "I'm a professional, don't try this at home." Then turned his truck down the hill and sped away...

REFERENCES

108. [Photo]

Sara's Guest House (Los Angeles County,
California)
intheeternal.com/en/id/433

18

Retreat

*"We must pass through solitude and
difficulty, isolation and silence, to find
that enchanted place where we can
dance our clumsy dance and sing our
sorrowful song. But in that dance, and
in that song, the most ancient rites
of our conscience fulfill themselves
in the awareness of being human."*

Toward the Splendid City

After Christmas, Dr. Chen took the girls snowboarding at Lake
Tahoe. I decided to stay home and have my own private retreat.
The first time I did a home retreat was in October 2001, after my
mother past away. My friend, David, called every hour or two. I
told him to leave me alone, but he said, "No, I want to make sure
you're okay."

"I'm fine. I just wanted to be alone."

"Don't lie! The calmer you are the more I know you're not okay."

So I turned off my cell phone and unplugged the house phone.
That afternoon, he came knocking on my door with his dog. I told
him that Buddhists often go on retreat to deal with personal issues.
I thought, "Actually, I don't have to go to a temple for retreat, I can
do it at home." There are many similarities between Buddhism and
Judaism, so he understood. He stayed for a while so I could play

with his dog. Animals, especially well behaved dogs and cats, have healing power.

He left after I agreed to give him a call whenever I needed emotional support. "If there's something you want to talk about, I am always available." He reiterated before getting into his truck. Watching him driving away, tears came drizzling down my cheeks. Grateful for his friendship and concern, I decided to put aside my sadness, and really started my private retreat.

On the third morning, the golden sunlight woke me up from my meditation. Outside the window, under clear blue sky and white clouds, the spicy aromatic fall air accompanied by the colorful leaves, reached out to me. I realized that I hadn't been outside for a few days, so I got out of bed and went for a drive. I drove to Starbucks for coffee, and then went to the bookstore at the other side of the parking lot. Dan Millman's *Way of the Peaceful Warrior*[110] fell off the bookshelf into my hand. I went home and read it nonstop, with little sleep, for two days.

"The world's a puzzle; no need to make sense out of it."

"Your business is not to 'get somewhere' – it is to be here."

"Use whatever knowledge you have but see its limitations. Knowledge alone does not suffice; it has no heart. No amount of knowledge will nourish or sustain your spirit; it can never bring you ultimate happiness or peace. Life requires more than knowledge; it requires intense feeling and constant energy. Life demands right action if knowledge is to come alive."

"Everyone tells you what's good for you. They don't want you to find your own answers. They want you to believe theirs. You can live a whole lifetime never being awake."

"The time is now, the place is here. Stay in the present. You can do nothing to change the past, and the future will never come exactly as you plan or hope for."

"You have been immortal since before you were born and will be long after the body dissolves. The body is Consciousness; never born; never dies; only changes. The mind — your ego, personal beliefs, history, and identity — is all that ends at death."

"For now, just think of death as a transformation—a bit more radical than puberty, but nothing to get particularly upset about. It's just one of the body's changes. When it happens, it happens. The warrior neither seeks death nor flees from it."

"Embrace the higher truth that everything comes to pass exactly as it should. Find peace and wisdom by accepting what is."

That retreat, especially Dan Millman's book, helped me get over the grief of losing my mother. Afterwards I bought several Dan's other books, and joined his readers' club.

At the beginning of 2006, before the movie "Peaceful Warrior" came out in the theater, I received an email from Dan. He stated that the movie will be released soon, and to show the appreciation for his readers, he would like to offer us free tickets.

I asked my daughters if they would go see a movie with me, as my birthday gift.

"Sure!" Yuan-Yuan said readily.

"Wait, which movie?" Xiang-Xiang asked cautiously.

"Well, it's not your typical movie. I don't think you heard of it."

"See! Don't agree so quickly." Xiang-Xinag told her sister, "Mommy is weird, I'm not sure if I want to watch some weird movie."

The two girls began to ask questions. I tried to answer as clearly as I could. Finally, I heard Yuan-Yuan whispered to her sister, "It's only two hours, if we don't like the movie, we can just take a nap."

Because it was not a mainstream movie, the nearest theater showing it was in Brea. When they were small I had to bribe them to come shopping with me, and one of the bribes that always worked was to have lunch at the restaurant in the Nordstrom department store.

After eating, they were satisfied and started joking and giggling just like usual. When we got to the theater, they only asked for a small drink, and were pretty much ready to take a nap. However, to their surprise, the movie was interesting and entertaining.

The young actors were very cute, and Nick Nolte was funny, even though the story line and thought provoking conversations in the movie were limited when compared with the original book. As inspirational and stimulating as the movie was, I was not sure how much those teenage girls really understood. At least they enjoyed watching it, and didn't fall asleep.

After the DVD was released, I bought three copies, to repay Dan for his free tickets. When Xiang-Xiang went to college a year later, she brought some DVDs with her to school, and this was one of them. What she didn't know, and what none of us would know, was that years later, one of her friends was stressed out in medical school. It was this movie that reminded him, "Don't let anyone tell you that you are not good enough!"

Los Angeles, California
December 2009

Seann came and left, and I didn't bother to explain as the kids were distracted with holiday parties. So, it seemed like business as usual in our household. Dr. Chen figured that I was probably not happy, and left me alone. The girls kept arguing with me, hoping I would give in and go with them to Lake Tahoe. But, I insisted that I wanted to stay home to relax, so they left with their dad happily.

After sending them off, I drove to buy a cup of coffee, and then went to the bookstore. We live in a very fortunate time. On the internet, all kinds of information is at our fingertips, but for me, it can not replace a real bookstore.

For many years, bookstores have been my sanctuary. No matter what kind of difficulty, challenge, or frustration I encountered, I could always go to a bookstore, see which book fell off the shelf, and usually, that book would provide some answers or clues that I needed to know.

That day I wandered around, but all of the books seemed sitting firmly on the shelves, so I decided to leave. On the way out I walked past the row of books on sale in front of the store, and accidentally bumped one and it fell to the floor. I bent down to pick it up from the ground.

It was *Jonathan Livingston Seagull*[111] by Richard Bach.

I had read the Chinese version in high school, and even though I didn't remember anything, there was a vague sense that there was something profound about that story. I went to the counter and paid for it, then went home. Turned on the heater, I crawled into bed under the comforter with a real sense of satisfaction. I opened the little book, and read nonstop until the last period. Then I closed my eyes and tried to meditate, but soon fell into sleep...

Jonathan Livingston Seagull

In my dream, Jonathan was transformed into a wise old man
with white hair and long white beard. We were walking on
the beach. He said, "Do you have any idea how many
lives we must have gone through before we even got the
first idea that there is more to the life we are living?"

"When you meet people and get to know them, if you only
remember the beautiful moments from the encounters, all those
loving feelings will stay in your heart forever and ever,
spiraling upwards..." He pointed his hand towards the sky"

"Life's twists and turns are full of surprises if you could look at
them from a different perspective. There are no boundaries,
no predicaments, no mandates on love. Love simply is."

"Do your best in every situation. No need to worry
about the result. For whatever you give, the
Universe always return it back to you three-fold."

"Don't believe what your eyes are telling you. All they
show is limitation. Look with your understanding. Find
out what you already know in your heart," he held
his hand over his heart for a moment then released
it toward the ocean , "and you will see the way..."

"You have the freedom to be yourself, your true self,
here and now, and nothing can stand in your way."

"...overcome space, and all we have left is Here.
Overcome time, and all we have left is Now. And in the
middle of Here and Now, we might meet again..."

He stopped and looked at me intensely. I
turned and looked back at the footprints on
the beach, how come there were only mine?

I woke up suddenly. Inside and outside, the whole house was pitch
black. I turned on the lights. They should be in Lake Tahoe by
now I thought and turned on my cell phone. There were missed
calls from Seann and Xiang-Xiang. Despite his sometimes indecisive

demeanor, Seann has always been reliable and trustworthy. I think that's why our friendship lasted.

I called Xiang-Xiang first, so that she wouldn't yell at me, "Why do you need a cell phone if you don't have it on or with you?"

"Mommy!" She said excitedly, "It's so beautiful here! The house Daddy rented is great! ...We miss you. I think you should buy a plane ticket and fly here."

I smiled, grateful for her sweetness and thoughtfulness, but I really needed the time alone.

After the divorce, I encouraged Dr. Chen to rebuild his own life, so every year he would go ski with his colleagues. My daughters are all athletes, so they are pretty good at snowboarding. In Los Angeles, we could get to the nearest ski area in a little over an hour, and their dad would sometimes take them to Mammoth to snowboard. But, this was the first time he took them to Lake Tahoe.

I grabbed the cold coffee from the night stand and went downstairs to feed the dogs. Just before I sat down at the breakfast table, the phone rang. I decided not to answer.

Over the years, I had friends call me all the time. I was a good listener, and I never gossiped. Anyone's secrets went in the trash after I hang up the phone. What bothered me was that I didn't know how to help them solve their problems. Many years later, I finally figured out that they didn't really want to solve the problems they were facing. Deep down, they may not even really be bothered by the problem they fussed about. It was just a habit of complaining.

Spouses, bosses, business, health, kids or no kids, everyone faces different challenges. When we focus on the problem, it becomes bigger and bigger, eventually too big to come up with any resolution. The only way to find the answer is change our perspective.

So all those years, although I had good intentions, trying to help my friends, by listening to their complains, I actually made things worse. Contemplating the words from Jonathan, "Life's twists and turns are full of surprises when viewed from a different perspective."

At that moment, my mind cleared. I don't need to know the future, I don't need to relive the past, and I don't need to have all the answers!

REFERENCES

109. [Photo]
Retreat (Malibu, California)
intheeternal.com/en/id/829

110. [Book]
Millman, D. (1980) Way of the Peaceful Warrior
intheeternal.com/en/id/817

111. [Book]
Bach, R. (1970) Jonathan Livingston Seagull
intheeternal.com/en/id/513

19

Return to Innocence

"The only task in your life and mine
is the restoration of our Identities
back to their original state of
void or zero."

— Dr. Ihaleakala Hew Len

Yangmingshan, Taiwan
July 2012

"The master at the temple asked why I haven't brought my friends who are staying in the Bed and Breakfast down the road to visit." Mason said, "Would you be interested?"

"Of course." Seann agreed right away, as he always enjoyed visiting temples.

From our Bed and Breakfast at Zhuzihu (Bamboo Lake), we could clearly see the Buddhist temple halfway up the hill. Seann was curious and asked about it a few times, but I just ignored him. Now the Master took the initiative and asked Mason to bring us to see him. "That's a little weird" I thought, not sure what to expect.

Religion has always been a sensitive topic.

Seann's mother was from a French-American heritage, and his father's family was from Texas. He followed his mother from Catholicism to Christianity, but always had a strong aversion to the traditions of Western religious beliefs. He resonated with the teachings of Jesus, but not the religion that had formed around them.

On the way to church one Sunday morning when he was about eight years old, he asked his mother, "If every religion says that God is on their side, how can you be sure that you are right? Is it possible that all of them are right, or maybe all of them are wrong?"

While his classmates were busy chasing girls, he was hiding in the library, reading a variety of books and magazines. When he was 16 he went to live with his free spirited father. In an environment with no specific religious beliefs, he studied a wide range of philosophies and psychology, plus ancient Chinese doctrines such as Lao Tzu and I Ching.

Even though we grew up poor, my mother never said no to my request for buying books. I was not interested in shopping, but I loved bookstores. From historical Chinese stories to biographical literature, to modern Kung Fu Jungle novels. From "Pride and Prejudice" to "The Count of Monte Cristo". I read variety of books, anything I could get my hands on. Unfortunately, I don't have a good memory and hardly remember much what I read. I have read more than ten books by master Nan Huaijin, but I only remember half of one poem he wrote.

> "We will all become ashes one day and realize that we are only guests passing through, Is there any point to calculate if we were winning or losing based on what we possessed?"

In the mid-1990s, the day before a trip back to Taiwan, I received an Express mail from my high school friend Mason. She asked me to find *Celestine Prophecy* and *Tenth Insight* for her. Since then, I have been fascinated with New Age books. And, I am now willing to accept that there is a much bigger world out there, much of it beyond my comprehension.

For as long as I could remember, whenever I saw my father, he always had a book in his hand. The first book he wrote took 17 years, "The Integral Theory of Mind and Matter[78]", and won the "Zhongshan Academic Award". He valued Chinese culture and theologies as a way to understand the nature of life. However, my father considered Buddhism to be superstitious, and did not spend much time looking at it. Later in life, his attitude towards Buddhism changed.

My parents eventually immigrated to the US and lived with us in Los Angeles. One day when I came home from work, my father was holding a book by a Buddhist author Feng Feng and said excitedly, "Mei-Mei (my nickname), this book is good, I've become enlightened today! Hahaha!" Although I did not have my father's comprehension and did not reach enlightenment that day, I was influenced by Feng Feng and became a vegetarian.

My mother said her life was saved by a Catholic hospital, so she called herself a Catholic. When we were young, she would take us to church in town occasionally. After they immigrated to the US and moved in with us, the local Christian church came knocking on our door and volunteered to drive them to attend church activities. Later my mother even persuaded my father to be baptized, which seemed to add a lot of peace and joy in their old age.

Yangmingshan, Taiwan
July 2012

It was a beautiful sunny day, and Mason arrived early. We finished eating breakfast hurriedly and followed her to the temple. The lady in charge of temple reception was Mason's junior high school classmate, and was very nice to us. She said that the Master rarely receives outsiders, and that we were a special case. To our great surprise, the first thing the Master talked about after he took his seat

Taiwan - YangMingShan

was Dr. Joe Vitale's book, Zero Limits[114]. The book is about the traditional Hawaiian spiritual healing practice, Ho'oponopono[115], which cleanses the mind and removes negative karmic obstacles.

Ho'oponopono is an ancient Hawaiian practice of forgiveness and reconciliation. Base on Dr. Ihaleakala Hew Len's teaching, the word "ho'o" means "cause" in Hawaiian, while "ponopono" means "perfection".

According to Dr. Vitale, Ho'oponopono is an inside out approach to change. Everything we see in the outside world, we can affect or influence by working on ourselves, because everything is interconnected. As above so below. Right!

Ho'oponopono can be thought of as a chant or prayer of four phrases, not necessarily in any specific order.

"I am sorry,
Please forgive me,
Thank you,
I love you!"

Dr. Joe Vitale is one of the people interviewed in the extremely popular documentary, *The Secret*[116]. When he heard the story about Dr. Ihaleakala Hew Len, a psychologist who cured all the criminals in a mental hospital without meeting any of them one on one, he visited Dr. Hew Len to confirm that incredible story. That meeting led to the book *Zero Limits*.

In the book, Dr. Ihaleakala Hew Len says that when he faced the patient, his own fear, hatred, sadness, confusion, shame and other negative emotions were all provoked by the patient. He realized that he had to cleanse himself of those negative emotions, before he could treat his patients. When looking at the patient's file and chanting the mantra, Dr. Ihaleakala Hew Len is cleaning up his own negative perceptions and feelings toward the patient.

At the hospital. he would take each patient's file and began to chant, "I'm sorry, please forgive me, I love you, thank you!" That made him feel better, and the patients got better. Ultimately, within a relatively short period of time, they started to be released by the hospital.

It is important to understand that with Ho'oponopono, the prayer is not about cleansing others. It is a practice that cleanses the negative memories or feelings that our body and mind holds, which purifies our consciousness.

I'm sorry, I don't know where all your painful negative emotions come from.

I'm sorry. Maybe I did something unconsciously to hurt you. Maybe it was my ancestors or society that did it.

Please forgive me for all the harm I have done to you by me or my ancestor's unconscious words and actions.

Thank you for being part of my life. Thank you for showing me what's in me that needs to be cleaned. Let's cleanse the pain of the past together!

And "I love you!" symbolizes a return to "Divine state" of perfection, it takes us back to ZERO. As Dr. Hew Len put it, "The Love will take you home, to pure state, to God/Divinity."

The method is simple yet powerful.

After discussing "Zero Limits" with the Master monk that day, I spent some time reading and practicing Ho'oponopono. Over the years, whenever my mind was in turmoil and I couldn't meditate, I would recite these mantras. Sometimes there was a specific person or object I focused on, and sometimes there wasn't, and I simply prayed for my own self-forgiveness. Occasionally, no matter how I would try, I couldn't say "I love you" to the so called 'bad guy' who was the object that caused my suffering.

Finally I learned that it's not 'I' who 'loves you'. The 'I' had to be transformed from the small ego based self, into a Universal Spirit or a God-like self. The small personality self only needed to get out of the way, because our conscious mind, the intellect, has no ability to erase the negative memories.

Dr. Ihaleakala Hew Len pointed out that when we say, please forgive me, we are praying to the Divine. As soon as we say I love you, a connection is made to the Divinity instantly. So when we say I love you, we're petition to Divine for repentance and forgiveness. There's nothing out there. We are 100 percent responsible for everything that happens in our awareness.

Dr. Ihaleakala Hew Len stated, "We are already perfect. The only purpose for me is to be memory free. To walk back to the essence, the essence is nothing. If we see anything which causes us to feel negative emotion, the problem is in me, in my memory. I am stuck in thinking. My job is just to work on me."

If we are responsible for everything that happens in our life, and are aware that all our feelings affect the outer world, it doesn't make sense to focus on other people or situations. The outside world will only change when our inner landscape is transformed. All the work is done in us. Nothing is out there.

Dr. Ihaleakala Hew Len clarified that, "Chaos is memory replaying in the subconscious (memory bank). When the conscious mind gets hooked into the chaos, it is stuck. At zero, when we are clear, we get what is right and perfect for us. And that is where inspiration comes. This process is to awaken yourself. And in that process, everything else get cleaned. Just like walking into a dark room, as you decide to clean and forgive, the light comes on for your entire world."

This simple practice can't really be effectively explained, it has to be experienced. Following is a Ho'oponopono prayer meditation done by Dr. Ihaleakala Hew Len, which to me is the most powerful and effective practice worth sharing.

"I love you. I love you. I'm sorry. Please forgive me for all the accumulated memories that you experience as sorrow, as grieving, as pain. I love you. Please forgive me for all the accumulated woes that you now have stored in you. I love you. Thank you. And I'm sorry if I've been neglectful, if I'm not taking good care of you, if I manipulated you, I'm sorry."

"Please let go of the memories that are replaying this. I don't know what the memories are, I don't want to know what the memories are, but you know. And then we can offer it to the Divinity, through the superconscious. We can ask the divinity to set it free."

"I love you and I'm sorry for all the accumulated memories that you experience as pain and suffering. Please, please forgive me. I'm sorry. Please, please forgive me. I love you. It just the memories that are the problem. I'm asking you to let go. Please let go. Please let go. Please let go. Thank you. I love you. I love you. Thank you for being willing to let go so that you and I can be memory free. You and I can walk hand in hand with the Divinity into the light."

Sara and Seann-Yangmingshan

Yangmingshan, Taiwan
July 2012

Even though Seann and I were enjoying the conversation with the Master monk, Mason was not interested in this topic. She seemed anxious to help Seann learn more about Buddhist practices and teachings. As soon as there was a break in the conversation, she asked the Master monk if he could explain certain knowledge or some specific Buddhist practices to Seann. He looked at Seann and said to Mason, "No need, he already knows." Mason looked at me in confusion, and I shrugged my shoulders. Maybe, truth is the same regardless how it's presented, and that all dharmas take us where we need to be.

After two hours of being a translator, I could see my own limitations. I understand English, but I had hard time translating it to Chinese. I know Chinese, but I couldn't translate it to English very well either. The good thing is that Seann understood my broken English perfectly, and Mason understood my broken Chinese and could help explain to the Master. Before we left, I offered a red envelope to the Master, but he pushed it back to me and said, "Save it for your travel expenses." I was baffled. Travel expenses? We didn't plan to leave Taiwan anytime soon.

REFERENCES

112. [Photo]

Innocence (Yangmingshan)

intheeternal.com/en/id/830

78. [Note]

PoTa Chou : About

intheeternal.com/en/id/531

113. [Photo]

Yangmingshan (Yangmingshan, Taiwan)

intheeternal.com/en/id/484

114.

[Book]

Vitale, J. & Len, I. H. (2007) *Zero Limits*

intheeternal.com/en/id/796

115.

[Link]

Ho'oponopono : *website*

intheeternal.com/en/id/797

116.

[Link]

The Secret : *Wikipedia page*

intheeternal.com/en/id/798

117.

[Photo]

Sara and Seann Yangmingshan
(Yangmingshan, Taiwan)

intheeternal.com/en/id/485

20

Reincarnation

*"How many of our previous lifetimes
ended with our dreams not realized?
Even though time and place has
changed, and we look a little different,
I still remember you!"*

— Author

Taipei, Taiwan
August 2012

We were planning to visit Taiwan's east coast, but a typhoon headed for that area ruined Seann's interest. And unfortunately, my Qigong teacher and my sister from previous lifetimes, were nowhere to be found.

Right after we left Yangmingshan to stay with a friend in Taipei, Seann was asked to help with another programming project. He needed some time to focus on programming, and being a guest in someone's home would make working difficult.

After I showed Seann an article about Hua Hin, Thailand, he became very interested and started researching Thailand. A few hours later, we decided that was the next stop on our trip. "That's the travel..." I poked Seann, "Remember the master gave me back the red envelope?"

I explained to my friends that we were going to Thailand, and told them that we would come back to visit more later. Since meeting Seann I had learned to expect the unexpected, and trust that things would work out in the end. That trip in Taiwan, being with Seann and my old friends and college classmates at the same time, made me realize how much I had changed since we met.

Albuquerque, New Mexico

Albuquerque, New Mexico
July 2009

At the Albuquerque workshop, after the bindi matching session, I invited Seann to go to dinner with some other students from the workshop. Marco invited me to ride in his car and Arturo invited Seann to ride in his car.

At dinner, there were several women who were very curious about Seann. One of them, a very friendly and beautiful young woman, even insisted that Seann was her brother in a previous life. Later, she said that in another lifetime, they had been husband and wife.

The next afternoon, Seann said to me, "Let's not go to dinner with anyone else tonight, okay? I have had enough talk of past lives for one weekend." So we went to a Vietnamese vegetarian restaurant, and talked way past the restaurant's closing hour.

"Take your time!" The owner brought a freshly brewed pot of tea, "I just wanted to tell you that the front door is locked. When you're ready to leave, let me know so I can open the door for you."

After thanking the owner, Seann refilled his tea cup and mine, clearly not having any intention of leaving. "During your travel to China, have you ever been to the Forbidden City?" He suddenly asked.

"I went there once with my friend David."

"What did you think about it?"

"I didn't like it very much. A very unhappy place." I was silent for a while. "Too much pain and suffering."

"Have you seen the movie, The Last Emperor?"

"Yes. It's a sad movie." The sadness almost brought back the pain in my heart. I've had chest pains occasionally ever since I was a kid.

"I liked it so much that I bought the DVD, and have watched it many times." He said.

I didn't respond and drank my tea in silence.

"There is an indescribable familiarity," he said. "I actually had a feeling that maybe I have lived there before, it's strange."

I felt that we were approaching a danger zone. "It's late, we should go." I didn't want to open that Pandora's Box.

We were still talking when we got back to the hotel, but it was late so we just went inside. As we were walking down the corridor, my room came first. I stopped by the door, watching him walking away in a commanding way...my chest ached again.

"Hey, my room is here." I called out to him, and he stopped and turned to say good night. I went in, showered and went to bed. I tried to tell myself that there was nothing unusual going on, and tried to get rid of the unexplained uneasiness in my heart.

— 今 —

The next morning, I was cleaning up my truck in the parking lot, moving snacks and drinks to the back so that I could have room to take Seann and another student to visit the workshop teachers' ranch.

"Good morning!" Seann came out of nowhere. "So, last night...," he paused for a second then anxiously continued, "Something unusual happened..."

"What are you talking about?" I said, trying to gain my composure, quickly smoothing my hair and turning to face him.

"I had a dream, well it was kind of a dream..." with a heavy look on his face, he murmured sadly, "Someone drowned in a box, and it was my fault."

Seeing his eyes were red and puffy, so I asked, "Have you been crying?"

He nodded, "I woke up in the middle of the night remembering that scene, and cried for over an hour. I actually buried my face in my pillow, so I wouldn't wake anyone up. I have never felt so much sorrow, it was very intense." He said, his eyes were watering again.

"Don't take it too seriously, whatever it was, it's not your fault!"

"You don't understand... First, I rarely remember my dreams, and secondly, I don't usually get emotional. This is not a normal thing at all. Maybe it was an emotional release of some kind, but I don't really understand what caused it."

"So... what do you mean a person was drowned? What kind of box?"

"I don't know. I just remember it was a small enclosed space. Maybe it wasn't a box, but that is kind of what it felt like, a small enclosed space, and water..." He looked dreary, "I don't understand, I have never felt such intense sadness."

"It's just a dream, don't worry about it. People die all of the time!" I tried to comfort him.

Later that afternoon, when leaving the ranch, we volunteered to take another student to the airport. Seann's flight was later in the evening, "My plane doesn't leave for another few hours, do you want to get something to eat?"

There were a few restaurants near the airport, and we chose "International House of Pancakes". Seann's grandmother would always make him pancakes when he visited. He felt the need for something sweet, and so did I.

As we were talking, he suddenly said, "I wonder if the dream I had was somehow related to our conversation last night?"

I was stunned and didn't say anything, he asked again, "You don't want to talk about your experience visiting the Forbidden City?"

I froze for a while. We'd only known each other for three days! But he was pressing, so I decided to tell him.

"I have had two recurring dreams since I was a child. In one of them, I crouched at the base of a wall and was crying uncontrollably. The wall was very high, very high, not just any wall. It was so high that I couldn't see the top. I knew I wasn't in prison, but I couldn't leave. It was a black and white dream, no color."

Seann looked at me intently with those beautiful blue eyes.

"The year my friend David and I went to the Forbidden City, we bought our tickets and walked to the entrance, the 'Noon Gate', and suddenly I realized that was the wall in my dream. I was crying there, in the dream, because I was outside and couldn't go in..."

"I kept crying and crying, and then an old man with a long white beard came and asked me to go with him. I refused, crying, "What will he do among those wolves without me?"

"I kept crying, and the old man sat there calmly waiting for me. When I stopped crying, trying to catch my breath, he said, ''If you want to help him, you have to come with me."

Seann waited patiently for me to continue, finally asking "And then what?"

I didn't answer, and the scene appeared in front of me again. It had been so many years, but everything was still so clear ...

David had gone with the tour guide, but suddenly realized that I was not behind him. He came back and found me standing by a pillar crying. He waited quietly for me to stop crying and said to me, "It looks like you know this place. We don't have to go with a tour guide, you can show me around."

We wandered into an exhibition hall, and suddenly I saw a portrait of Emperor Guangxu, "That's not right!" I said, frustrated, "That doesn't look like him at all!"

"I guess you know this guy, eh?" David said jokingly.

I came back to reality. Just when Seann asked again anxiously. "What happened next?"

"I woke up."

"Huh. Well, I'm impressed, I don't remember any childhood dreams."

"I only dreamed of crying at the base of the wall when I was little, I didn't understand what it meant. The old man and the other scenes..., they only started after I visited Forbidden City... It was so vivid and clear."

I looked up at Seann. His face was turned to the side, his eyes were looking down, that look..., it felt like a heavy blow to my heart....

"You mentioned two recurring dreams. What about the second one?"

I sat motionless, not knowing how to respond.

"It's getting late, we need to get to the airport. We can talk about it later." I said, trying to avoid discussing it.

On the drive back to Sedona, that whole lifetime played like a flash back, in front of my open eyes.

Santa Rosa, California
April 2011

After we moved to Santa Rosa, we spent a lot of time exploring Northern California, and even more time talking. The villa had a hot tub and a nicely landscaped backyard, so it was a great place to spend cool winter nights and warm spring afternoons.

One morning we were talking...

"Whenever we have been involved in the past, we are on the same journey." I said, trying to summarize what I had been thinking when waking up that morning. "We are both searching for enlightenment, for answers. So every time we meet, we continue our journey. A lot of the time we were involved, we were trying to do things, not just for us. We were trying to find solutions for everyone. And that's why we gravitated to each other."

He nodded. "Around 2007, Hans King said my work would be drawn to me over the next 3-4 years. That's the way he said it, 'it would be drawn to me'. When I really committed to make my spiritual life the first priority, when I rented the cabin in North Carolina, that is when we met. We were drawn together."

We sat and sipped coffee, watching the sun peeking out from the clouds, highlighting the colors of the flowers in the backyard.

"It makes so much sense, the first time you talked to Ahtun Re, he brought up the lifetime 600 years ago. Zhu Gong[56] had ideas about a lot of things, including architecture. Ming Xiaoling was built based on his designs.

And, Zhu Di also used that design for the Forbidden City. The other day we looked at the information that's available for Ming Xiao Ling online, and just like Ahtun Re said, it looks like Zhu Gong's work. So, Zhu Di took your work, and built the Forbidden City."

Ming Xiaoling, Nanjing

"Zhu Di took Zhu Gong's work, not mine." Seann interjected. "We shouldn't say 'me' when talking about the past, we are different personalities, even though we share the same soul."

"I know, but it's just us talking, you know what I mean. So anyway, the thing you showed me, the way they built the walls and you had to come in through one side and then go around...when we go to China we also need to go to Shanxi province."

I grabbed my notebook and added Shanxi[120] to the list of places to visit. Zhu Gong's father, Emperor Hongwu, made him Prince of Jin, and Shanxi was his territory.

"You know, when I was a kid, I used to draw structures. For instance, there would be a hill, and I would draw all of the support structures to enable a building to extend out over a hillside. I used to draw buildings and forts, and it...it makes sense now." he said, getting into a reflective mode. "And, remember our conversations about the shortsightedness of building cities in places where the environment can't naturally support many people?"

"Yeah, you mentioned that a lot when we were in LA." I would sometimes get frustrated when he would make those kinds of comments, but after living in the mountains of Northern California, I began to understand what he meant.

"Even before our first session with Ahtun Re, we talked about the Feng Shui of houses and buildings we would see when driving around. Anyway, you know what I am saying. I always paid attention to that kind of thing, and now it makes sense where that came from."

We sat in silence for a few minutes, then he got up, "More coffee?"

"Sure."

He brought the french press from the kitchen, pouring a little more coffee in our cups.

"It was kind of the same with me." I said, remembering some of my childhood. "My mom told me I was naturally a good singer. When I was only three I could sing a song after listening to it just once. And, I also played Pi-Pa in college. That didn't come naturally, but wasn't difficult either."

Sara - Pipa

"When I first arrived in Santa Barbara to attend graduate school at UCSB, I was so mesmerized by the beauty of the campus. For two weeks I would wander around the campus and write instead of attending classes and studying. That turned into a novel, and was published in the World Journal. But, I nearly flunked out that quarter, because there's only 10 weeks plus final week in each quarter."

"The World Journal? Is that the Chinese newspaper we see in Asian supermarkets?"

"Yeah. The editor in chief for the Journal wrote me a letter, encouraging me to keep writing... And, of course I didn't. I'm not good at writing about just any topic, I can only write about something that is inspiring or interesting to me. In other words, if it wasn't my focus, it would be hard for me to accomplish anything just by working hard."

"Yeah, me either. But, the point is, you brought those talents and abilities with you, from previous lifetimes. Not everyone can write, or play musical instruments and sing."

"But I don't want to focus on those things, that is not important!" Ever since I was young, the last thing I wanted was to glorify my ego.

"It is important because it illustrates a point. It's not about you, or me, I am not saying we are special. It shows that what we learn, and the efforts we make to become better people, enrich our soul. And, we take that with us into our next life. It's never too late to start, because our journey continues after this life." He said emphatically.

"We need to focus on who we are now, not who we have been. I want to understand why we are here, how can we create a more meaningful life, and not just for ourselves. Those things are more important!" I said, still not totally comfortable with the conversation.

"I agree," he said, patiently. "Everyone eventually gets to the point that they search for deeper meaning. But, it's still good to try and create meaningful things in the world. Like you said, the goal is making things better for everyone, not just ourselves." He looked out the window at the flowers, before finishing his thoughts.

"Eventually everyone gets to that point, the only question is how long we make ourselves and those around us suffer before we wake up and remember."

Before we went to China, we had several more sessions with Kevin and Ahtun Re, to clarify a few more details about our past...

Seann had a long list of questions, and started with a subject we had spoken about several times. "In the lifetime that ended 100 years ago there was a person, the head Eunuch...Li Lianying. There was a strong dislike, and some conflict between my personage in that life, and him."

"Are there surviving photographs of this fellow?" Ahtun Re asked.

Seann hesitated, "Yes. He was, um, very unattractive. He is a shorter man, dark complexion, deep wrinkles, not a pleasant looking person."

Li Lianying

"One moment... I think he was a younger brother of yours in one of those other monarchial lifetimes." Ahtun Re replied. "And, he sort of always resented being at the end of the line of inheritance. And to make matters worse, he was even born to a lesser mother, removing him even further."

Seann looked at me as if to ask, "Do you know what he means?" I shook my head.

Ahtun Re continued, "you might say his appearance was symbolic of his covetousness, and his shortness in stature would have made him the antithesis of a role model for royalty. Kind of like the portrait of Dorian Gray[123], except he was living it."

Now I looked at Seann, not knowing who Dorian Gray was. He smiled and held up his hand as if to say, "Hold on, I will explain."

"I think as a penance, and one that is probably working...I think he is among the monks that serve the Dalai Lama. There he finds the compassion and forgiveness that he was so desperately seeking, by living it. And, if you will, it is his own China that has exiled him. That's an interesting fate isn't it?"

Zhu Di

"Yes...it is." Seann replied.

Later when we were discussing this session with Ahtun Re, Seann reflected on his lifetime as Zhu Gong, and the conflict between him and his younger brother Zhu Di, the Usurper Emperor from the Ming Dynasty.

In a follow-up session with Kevin, Seann asked Ahtun Re if Zhu Di had reincarnated as the eunuch, Li Lianying.

"Yes, that would be accurate." Ahtun Re replied.

He continued, "You see, because he placed himself in the position of Emperor, his intention was to rise to the top...and in a way, the Eunuch can be incredibly powerful, with their power over the bureaucracy, but at the same time it is one of the humblest positions within the court. So, it is only fitting that the fellow who was there at the beginning should be there at the bookend, or the conclusion."

Seann looked at me while nodding his head in agreement.

"You might say, in that earlier lifetime he prided himself on his lusty powers, so it was his karma to have the symbols of that, or the organs that it is associated with, removed."

Seann started to reply, slowly. "Yeah. So, that..."

Ahtun Re didn't wait for him to complete his sentence, "...and by the way, when this is all done, it would make a very nice story...about parallel lives."

We both agreed, but were stunned.

We also confirmed that Zhu Di's mother was not Empress Ma, but a concubine who was a Mongol Princess, making him half Mongol. So, it makes sense why Emperor Hongwu asked him to oversee the territory in North East China, as that region was near Mongol territory.

That also explains why Zhu Di eventually built the Forbidden City and moved the capital to what is now Beijing, because that is where he felt safe. Nanjing was the true capital, and therefore was full of people who might try to take back the throne, knowing he was a Usurper, and that his mother was a Mongol who came from the recently defeated Yuan Dynasty.

Even years later when re-listening to the recording, it is still a lot to process. In the case of Li Lianying, 500 years later he was living out the karma started in his life as the Usurper Emperor Zhu Di.

During my first session with Kevin and Ahtun Re, I asked about the Dowager Empress Cixi. My feelings about the lifetime as Pearl were strong, but Ahtun Re helped put it in perspective.

"I have very strong emotional reaction to her, when I eventually finally accepted the story... I am fine now, I am over that."

"That's good Buddhism. Non-attachment." Ahtun Re joked.

"Yes. I am clear now, but it took a long time and a lot of effort, but in this lifetime I always feel like there are dark shadows, hovering around me."

"In Egypt we used to say that if you were scared by a Camel's shadow one night, the actual Camel will still make you nervous. In a way you might say, the emotions or the shadows of that previous lifetime, are still with you. But this lifetime, is not living in the...how to put this... The aunt you might say, had a period of influence during the Chiang Kai-shek[125] period, and had lived something of a privileged existence. So I suppose to a certain degree, you lived still somewhat in the shadows of those autocratic ways. But your own psychic liberation, living among the progressive ways, but also...here is another key...

Even within the technological, political and sociologically progressive era, there is a part of you that is even living a deeper liberation that is a psychic liberation. So, without saying who exactly, there have been some prominent female figures in the Chiang Kai-shek era, who wielded political and economic power. I would go so far as to say that one of those was this aunt."

"Oh! Okay." I wasn't surprised, but was curious who she could be.

Eventually, Ahtun Re ended that discussion with, "I think you have stepped out of the shadow of the aunt, and you are living in the sunshine of your own existence."

"Yes, I am now."

Wondering who Ahtun Re might have been referring to, Seann did some research of prominent Chinese women during Chiang Kai-shek's time. One day, he saw a picture of Mao Zedong's wife, Jiang Qing, that caught his attention. After looking into her past and learning of her role in the Cultural Revolution, he became convinced she might be the reincarnation of Cixi, as there were some parallels between that and the Boxer Rebellion.

Cixi

Jiang Qing

In my next session with Ahtun Re, I asked.

"The answer is yes, that was her reincarnation." He responded, without hesitation.

"Yeah, they look alike."

"That is interesting isn't it? That is one of the attributes, one's energy anatomy does carry over one's physical appearance, and many mannerisms also."

Knowing that people's difficulties sometimes started many lifetimes ago, and understanding that our behavior could lead to that kind of outcome, it is more clear how important it is to act with integrity. In the long run, the consequences of our actions can either create a positive spiral upwards, or a negative downward spiral full of pain and suffering. The choice is ours.

REFERENCES

118. [Photo]
Wheel of Life (Chiang Mai, Thailand)
intheeternal.com/en/id/491

119. [Location]
Albuquerque, New Mexico
intheeternal.com/en/id/371

56. [Note]
Zhu Gong : Son of Hongwu Emperor
intheeternal.com/en/id/521

120. [Location]
Shanxi, China
intheeternal.com/en/id/382

121. [Photo]
Sara playing Pipa (UCSB)
intheeternal.com/en/id/483

122. [Image]
Li Lianying
intheeternal.com/en/id/514

123. [Link]
Dorian Gray : Wikipedia page
intheeternal.com/en/id/799

124. [Image]

Zhu Di

intheeternal.com/en/id/515

125. [Note]

Chiang Kai-shek : Chairman - National Government of China

intheeternal.com/en/id/520

126. [Image]

Cixi - Portrait

intheeternal.com/en/id/516

127. [Image]

Jiang Qing

intheeternal.com/en/id/517

21

Perseverance

"Unless we endure the
bone chilling snowy storm,
we would not have the fragrant
of plum blossoms to enjoy!"

— Author

Hua Hin, Thailand
August 2012

After arriving in Hua Hin, Thailand, one day we were walking on the beach. I told Seann happily, "Let's move here!"

"Really? You really want to move here?"

"Why not?" I said to him casually and didn't give it much thought. Ever since I arrived in California for graduate school, I have always lived close to the ocean. I loved California beaches, especially Malibu and Santa Barbara.

An old Chinese saying states,

"A benevolent man appreciates the mountains,
a wise man appreciates the water."

Although I love the ocean, I have always been afraid of sticking my head under the water. So, I guess I am not really a wise woman. Seann loves the mountains, and truly is a benevolent person.

That night at the hotel, I was reading travel information I had collected during the day. Seann was on his laptop, working on his new programming project. Pictures of the scenery around Chiang Mai showed rolling hills of greenery, rice fields, waterfalls and springs...

"Look, it's so beautiful there." I showed it to Seann.

"That's tourist marketing material, of course it's beautiful." He said, but stopped what he was doing and took the brochure.

"Those Hill Tribe people," he pointed to a picture, "They look like the Mayans in Guatemala."

I bent over to see the pictures, "Yeah, they do." The colorful clothes, and the way people look are really similar. It reminded me of the stories of previous advanced civilizations. Maybe the reason some people in Central and South America and Asia have similar physical features, clothing and customs, is because at one time they were the same people. There is a lot about history that we don't know, and a lot of what we think we know may not be entirely accurate.

Guatemala - Walking to the Market

Lake Atitlan, Guatemala
March 2010

After Seann moved to Los Angeles, we processed some of the emotional residue from previous lifetimes. Seann also quit smoking, which he said was easy because he didn't enjoy it anymore. His coming to LA was an adjustment for both of us, but we enjoyed being able to spend more time together, and I was able to show him some of my favorite southern California landmarks and beaches.

A month later, we decided to ask the teachers from Albuquerque, Doc and his wife, about our experiences. They had moved to Guatemala, and recommended that we sign up for an upcoming workshop and individual consultations so they could help us gain a deeper understanding of our past lives.

We made the trip to Guatemala, hoping to gain some clarity about what we had learned since meeting. In the end, Seann had some disagreements with the wife about several things.

I went in after Seann, not knowing what happened during his session, and was emotional as usual whenever talking about that lifetime . While I was crying my heart out, she told me,

"You are her reincarnation, but Seann was not the Emperor in that life." Doc looked at me with compassion, and his wife continued, "The Emperor did not reincarnate, he is in a higher realm, always watching over you."

"Always watching over me?" I asked, wiping my tears...

"Yes, he loves you very much and stays by your side all the time."

Then, I stopped crying, feeling a little uneasy in my stomach.

Their cottage was built on the shore of Lake Atitlan, outside of a small Mayan village, and was easier to access by boat. In the village they rented a separate western style house for students' accommodations. There was one other student besides the two of us having a consultation session at their cottage that day, so we rode in the boat together that morning.

At the end of the day, we were waiting for the boat to come while the other student was finishing her session. Seann walked down the hill alone, all the way to the lakeside. I stood in the garden halfway up the hill, looking out over the lake and the mountains.

"How is he?" Doc came up to me and pointed to Seann.

I was startled and replied reflexively, "I don't know... He doesn't look very happy, so I'd like to give him some space."

"Don't blame him. You're the only one who can help him get through this." Seeing that I was a little confused, Doc added, "He is a very wise and capable person, but someone convinced him that he was powerless..."

After a pause, Doc continued, "Tell him to listen to his own inner voice. The truth is in your hearts, and in fact, you already know it..."

"Trust the process!" He said as the the wind started blowing. Doc's long white hair, long white beard, and white robe were flowing in the breeze...

Student House

The three day private consultation leading up to the workshop had ended, and Seann was not happy with the way things were going.

We sat in silence, looking out of the sliding glass door at the lake. The boat had just dropped us off at the village. The house was quiet and still, we were alone. It was a beautiful sunny afternoon, but the seriousness of our situation was setting in. More students were arriving that afternoon for the workshop, and they wanted us to separate and share rooms with other people.

"So, can we not split up and share rooms with the people coming this afternoon?"

"I won't kick you out. Maybe we can talk with them?" I suggested.

Seann spoke with the workshop assistant on speakerphone. When he said Seann was causing conflicts between Doc and his wife, we looked at each other, "What the..." I whispered with frustration. Seann put his hand on my back to calm me down, telling the assistant he was not comfortable sharing a room with other people. We hoped they would agree since we came together, but when the assistant insisted that we would need to split up, Seann said he would leave before the other workshop participants arrived, to avoid any further disruption.

I couldn't just let him go alone, so we packed up and left together.

We checked in to a hotel in Panajachel, and both felt a sense of relief. The next day we contacted the local American guide, Ryan. His wife was a Mayan local, and he was able to arrange for us to meet with the local Mayan elder priest, Don Solsa. By the time we arrived, the house of Don Solsa was already full of locals, all of them waiting patiently, hoping to get his help with something.

A few days earlier, we had been invited to attend a special ceremony for Ryan and his Mayan wife's newborn baby. He asked Seann to be the photographer, and I helped take care of their three-year-old son.

Guatemala - Sara

At the end of the ceremony, everyone lined up and Don Solsa prayed for all the guests one by one. When it was Seann's turn, Don Solsa said, "Your future success is unlimited if you could resolve the problem in front of you."

Don was especially happy to see me. The "friends from afar" were of extraordinary importance to Mayans ceremony. China, which I represent, is a very distant place for them.

Perhaps it was because of that special encounter, that Ryan was able to lead us directly to Don Solsa's desk.

"So many people ahead of us." We were hesitant, not used to cut in line.

"They can come back tomorrow, unlike you." Ryan said, "They understand."

After reading our astrology, Don Solsa said he could help clear some of the old energy around us if we wanted his help. We agreed, and he asked us to step out the door behind his desk. A 1,200 year old stone altar was in the backyard, and his house was built around that huge stone.

He lit a fire in the center, placed various objects at different locations around the circular stone altar, lit candles and incense, then went into a trance like state. Ryan interpreted some of what was being said and relayed some questions, but we all mostly stayed silent, letting Don Solsa do his work.

Don told me to be careful, so I won't get injured working in the kitchen. That was true, I hardly ever cooked back then, and every time I went into the kitchen, something bad would happen. Either I would cut my hand or hit my head.

"You are the bridge between heaven and earth, your writing will help connect them." he told Seann. "But, that woman will do anything to stop you from succeeding." We weren't sure which woman he was referring to, maybe just left over energies from previous lifetimes.

When he finished his clearing ritual, we walked to the front of his house. Seann asked if Mayan's believed in reincarnation, and Don Solsa nodded his head before Ryan was finished, saying "Sometimes the ancestors return to bring things into the world, yes."

One thing I can say that came from the trip, was that I really did stop having accidents in the kitchen. As for Seann's problem, I don't know if it's solved, but I hope so.

Hua Hin, Thailand
August 2012

A few days after arriving in Hua Hin, Seann rented a motorbike and practiced riding around town a little. Once he felt confident, we began to explore some of the surrounding areas.

We visited some Temples, beaches, and found a market selling locally made goods. Thailand reminded me of what Taiwan was like when I was growing up, except for the monkeys and elephants.

The beach was mostly empty as we walked along the shore, letting the water wash over our feet. There were not a lot of seagulls

Thailand - Monkey Temple

and plenty of food around, and I remembered Jonathan Livingston Seagull. If he were in this relaxed, abundant, and noncompetitive environment, would he still strive to fly outside of self-imposed limitations, or contemplate ideas that are out of the normal daily routine?

> *"Do you have any idea how many lives we must*
> *have gone through before we even got the first*
> *idea that there is more to the life we are living?"*

Unexpectedly, his words appeared in my mind.

We walked in silence, occasionally looking at each other. We walked along the shore at Lake Atitlan in Guatemala too, but there is something special about the ocean.

"What are you thinking?" Seann brought me back to reality.

"Nothing. Just remembering Guatemala." I smiled at him, but in my heart I felt an inexplicable uneasiness.

He seemed to be sensing something, then abruptly turned to me and said intently, "Remember what Doc said, trust the process."

REFERENCES

128. [Photo]
Hua Hin (Hua Hin, Thailand)
intheeternal.com/en/id/489

129. [Location]
Hua Hin, Thailand
intheeternal.com/en/id/386

130. [Photo]
Walking to Market (Lake Atitlan, Guatemala)
intheeternal.com/en/id/469

131. [Photo]
Student House (Lake Atitlan, Guatemala)
intheeternal.com/en/id/470

132. [Photo]
Guatemala - Sara (Lake Atitlan, Guatemala)
intheeternal.com/en/id/472

133. [Photo]
Monkey Temple (Hua Hin, Thailand)
intheeternal.com/en/id/490

22

We Will Meet Again

"Don't be dismayed at good-byes.
A farewell is necessary before you
can meet again. And meeting
again, after moments or lifetimes, is
certain for those who are friends.'"

— Richard Bach - Illusions

That morning, when we were discussing whether we should go to Chiang Mai , I received a text message from Xiang-Xiang:

"Mommy, I just wanted to tell you that Bo-Bo was in a bad car accident. She is in surgery now. I think she's going to be okay."

I dropped my phone and started crying. Seann picked up my phone. After reading the text message he came over to hug me, trying not to get lost in my sadness.

After helping me calm down, Seann tried to get me mentally prepared for my trip home. "You need to focus on your daughter, my presence will distract you," he said. "I can go to Chiang Mai for now, and we will see how things go."

Later, he looked at me with a serious expression, "She might be hurt badly, so be prepared."

I knew he was probably right, Xiang-Xiang just didn't want me to worry.

"She will be okay. Don't focus on the current situation, imagine her a year from now." His voice was tenacious and firm. "When you meditate, focus your attention on the result. Don't let the difficulty of the process make you lose your spirit. It will all pass, she will recover."

We were both silent, reflecting on the situation. After we both meditated for a while, he touched my knee to get my attention.

"If you want to cry, do it in your car before you go into the hospital," he said, putting his hand over his heart. "If you want to help her, you have to keep your energy level high. Expect her to fully recover, hold that expectation, bring that energy into the room."

"She's your daughter, and you are a healer." He tried to reassure me. "Remember what you know, stay focused on a positive outcome. She will recover."

— 今 —

The morning after, we were in a taxi on the way to Bangkok airport. Silence filled the air grievously.

Is it safe to be a stranger in a foreign country by himself? I questioned, but did not have the emotional capacity to express my concern, so I just sat quietly, looking at the moving scenery out the window.

After I checked in, he pushed my carry on bag, walking me to the escalator. We hadn't talked much the whole way.

"I have to leave, security is upstairs and they are checking tickets at the escalator." I took over the luggage and was about to go upstairs when Seann pulled me into his arms, uncharacteristically. "You take care of yourself, okay." I leaned against his firm chest, and lowered my head to wipe my tears with my jacket.

"Think about bringing her to visit me in Chiang Mai a year from now, when she's fully recovered." He said.

"You're going to stay here?" I raised my head, dazed.

"Maybe. We'll see how it goes." After a long pause, he broke the silence, "When you arrive in San Francisco, call me."

I nodded reluctantly. Yesterday, while I was busy looking for tickets he made changes to our Internet phones, so we could talk wherever he would be. We spent most of the day in silence, the subject was too heavy.

"Remember who you are. The real you is not limited to this life, or this body..." he said.

At that moment, I realized his uneasiness. That's all he could do to help, the rest was up to me.

"I know. Don't worry about me, just come back when you have seen enough of Thailand." Wiping away my tears, I raised my head to look at him and tried to smile. "You have to take care of yourself while I'm gone, don't work on the computer past midnight every day."

He laughed, "Who's been taking care of who these past few years?"

"Okay, maybe both ways." I laughed too.

"I'll be waiting for your call," he patted my shoulder, "go on..."

I took a deep breathe, stepped onto the escalator. "Call anytime, don't be afraid to wake me up..." His voice was trailing behind my back.

I waved and motioned for him to go. When I got to the second floor, I stopped and watched him walking away. All of a sudden, I remembered a phrase I read somewhere.

"I will come back if I am alive.
If I die, our everlasting love will never be forgotten."

It's just as simple as that, is it?
Isn't it?

REFERENCES

134. [Photo]

BKK (Bangkok Airport)

intheeternal.com/en/id/835

Appendices

Afterward

Thanks to the amazing doctors and nurses, and with the help of countless prayers from my friends and their prayer groups, my brave daughter survived and fully recovered from the horrifying car accident.

In his famous 2005 Stanford University graduation commencement speech, Steve Jobs said,

> "You can't connect the dots looking forward; you can only connect them looking backwards. So you have to trust that the dots will somehow connect in your future. You have to trust in something – your gut, destiny, life, karma, whatever. This approach has never let me down, and it has made all the difference in my life."

The world is changing fast. We really can't plan the future based on our past experience, we just do the best we can and believe our efforts will grow into something beyond what we can imagine today.

After I met Seann, I wrote in my journal, "Knowing you exist, put my mind at ease." But I didn't really, truly get what I wrote until just now. Since we met, I have learned so much from Seann, while healing unconscious wounds accumulated from past lives.

There's an old Indian saying, people often need to walk three villages before they can find a guru, because we tend to undervalue people who are close to us. Through the process of writing this book, I have started to appreciate Seann wholeheartedly.

Even though I wrote the first version of the book, I only hinted at who we were in our previous lifetimes, and there was much less dialogue. Seann has participated throughout the process of making the book what it is now, as co-creator and editor of the finished work. Seann is also the original creator of the book's website, and is responsible for it's publication.

Over the years, we may disagree about some things...we disagree often, actually. But in the end, we always walk away with more clarity and a better understanding of the larger reality. The process hasn't been easy for us. We have had to face our deepest fears, and many issues that we didn't want to acknowledge. But, from where we sit now, it has been very rewarding.

And, once we accept the reality of reincarnation, time is no longer a limitation. Death is not the end, and birth is not the beginning. Life is a continuing process, spiraling up on our evolutionary journey as conscious beings.

LETTING GO

Here, I would like to share a little story about Buddhism. Someone once asked a Zen Master, "What have you gained through all your practice?"

The Zen Master answered, "Nothing."

"Then why are you willing to give up material possessions and worldly recognition to continue your practice?"

"Let me tell you what I have let go." The Zen Master said with compassion, "I have let go of negative preconceptions. I have also let go of my selfishness, greed, judgment, and attachment to this material world. Most importantly, I no longer have the fear of getting old, or death."

For us, we believe that the true purpose of Buddhist practice is not to gain anything, but to let go all of the non-beneficial energy we have been holding on to, in some cases for many lifetimes. Looking back from where I sit now, I too have let go of much of my anger, sorrow, worries, insecurity, fear, depression and anxiety. I have also let go of my egocentric self-identification, and made peace with myself.

In the process of preparing the manuscript for publication, I re-read *Zero Limits*[114], and watched a lot of lectures by Dr. Ihaleakala Hew Len. As a result, my understanding of his work is far more profound than it was eleven years ago.

We are all like children who have left home to embark on a journey. No matter how far we go, we will all return home one day. I believe that no one will take home the rubbish we have accumulated along the trip. Dr. Ihaleakala Hew Len points out that, since time immemorial, the memories accumulated in our subconscious, all the worries, pains, and negativity, prevent us from returning home.

Unfortunately, Dr. Hew Len had left this world in 2022. I would like to express deep gratitude for him and his work, as it gives us the opportunity to cleanse our body, mind and soul, and return to our original innocence.

It has taken 14 years for me to finally feel comfortable sharing our story publicly. A huge gratitude to Seann for his patience and persistence.

Lifetime after lifetime, we have played different roles. Some roles we might consciously volunteer for, and others we might gravitate to in order to resolve unfinished business. Sometimes we might have certain experiences in order to learn, grow, and transform, while some lifetimes are more like vacations, breaks we need to prepare for the next step forward.

The point is, no matter what role we play in our various lifetimes, they are all temporary manifestations from our soul. In a way, we are all like children who left home to embark on a journey to experience the outside world. No matter how far we venture into the physical realm, one day, we will all find our way back home.

It doesn't matter which path we take, eventually we will return to our original state of innocence.

Once we realize the path to true freedom is an inner journey, we just have to keep at it. Knowing that it may take many lifetimes to reach the ultimate goal we seek, eases the sense of urgency.

The end is just the beginning of the next step. In this ever changing, magical universe we share, I'm sure we will meet again!

Sara Chou
Lake Tahoe, California
August, 2018
Updated: September, 2023

REFERENCES

114.
[Book]

Vitale, J. & Len, I. H. (2007) *Zero Limits*

intheeternal.com/en/id/796

Reincarnation Research

As detailed in the Introduction, a few weeks after meeting Sara, she said I was Guangxu in a previous life. I have been interested in Eastern Philosophy since my teen years, and was fascinated with the movie *The Last Emperor*, so it wasn't such a strange idea. However, I needed some sort of evidence before accepting her story, and started researching what I could find online about Guangxu. Within a couple of days I discovered the portrait shown below, at which point I decided to take it seriously.

Guangxu Emperor

Seann in 1999

After reading some books about Guangxu, I found a lot of similar personality traits and interests. For instance, as a child I would take apart clocks and radios to how they worked, and spent my career designing electronic systems. When I read that Guangxu liked to tinker with clocks, and had both a telegraph and electricity installed in some parts of the Forbidden City, that caught my attention. It wasn't just the similar appearance that I shared with Guangxu, we also shared similar talents and interests.

It seemed Sara might be right, but then what? The Tibetans have techniques to identify reincarnated Lamas, so there is some understanding in their tradition, but has anyone written about the process? Are there other people who have told the story of how they learned about their previous lives? How did they integrate that into their worldview?

Those questions led to months of research, trying to find what I could online, in an attempt to understand how reincarnation actually works. If I were an Emperor 100 years ago, why was I born into a middle class family in Texas? Are such drastic changes in culture common? Do we reincarnate immediately after death, or are there large gaps in time? There was enough time between the death of Guangxu in 1908 and my birth in 1972 for there to be another lifetime, so maybe there was an 'in-between' lifetime that made the transition make more sense (there was), but how could I find out? The more I searched, the more questions I had...

WALTER SEMKIW

Then, I found the work of Dr. Walter Semkiw[137]. The case histories presented at his website, and his book *Origin of the Soul*[138] helped to answer most of the questions I had, and some I hadn't thought to ask. Interestingly enough, his research into reincarnation started after learning about one of *his* previous incarnations, as John Adams, the second President of the United States.

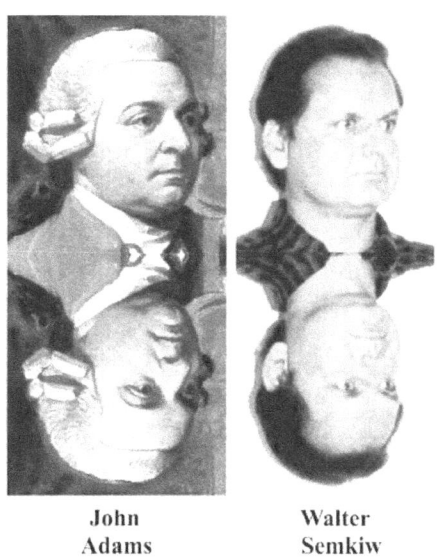

John   Walter
Adams   Semkiw

Adams - Semkiw

Dr. Semkiw's exploration of reincarnation expands on the work started by Ian Stevenson[140]. Walter had the benefit of being able to refer to Stevenson's work, but also the advantage of having more photographic evidence, and of course access to the internet. However, probably the biggest advantage Walter had over Stevenson, was being able to verify cases with the help of Kevin Ryerson.

KEVIN RYERSON

Kevin Ryerson[13], a trance channel in the tradition of Edgar Cayce, started to work with Dr. Semkiw back in 2001. The guides Kevin works with were able to identify and confirm many of the past life histories Walter was exploring, as shown in the Core Cases[141] highlighted on his website.

During the first session with Kevin (see Chapter 8), the spirit guide Ahtun Re confirmed that I was Guangxu, and mentioned another, related lifetime Sara and I shared over 600 years ago, at the beginning of the Ming Dynasty. Sara knew the history and the persons mentioned, which of course generated more questions. That session led to several others, each one building on the last, helping to clarify why Guangxu's life ended the way it did, and what led to him being in that situation in the first place.

Over the last 13 years, Sara and I have been able to piece together a broad overview of some of our previous lifetimes. That process has helped to illustrate how the events of each lifetime may continue into the next. And that who we are in any one lifetime, is the culmination of many, many life experiences over long periods of time.

MEETING KEVIN AND WALTER

I first met Kevin and Walter in 2011 at the East West Book-store in Mountain View, California. Over a couple of evenings, Walter presented some of the more compelling case histories, while highlighting some of the principles of reincarnation that he has observed.

At the end of the event, I approached the group of people standing around Walter asking questions, wanting to thank him. Someone had just asked about a historically significant person, to which Walter replied "you could be standing right next to the reincarnation of some notable historical figure, and you wouldn't know it." He made the point that for every life as a historically significant person, a soul has many more that are not necessarily all that special.

Meeting and speaking with Walter, and seeing Kevin's work in person, helped to clarify many of the questions I had developed up to that point. However, something interesting began to happen, which apparently happened to Walter also.

I started to have intuitive hunches that some of the people I knew, may have been involved in previous incarnations. And, I started identifying people that I *did not* know, and who *they* might have been before.

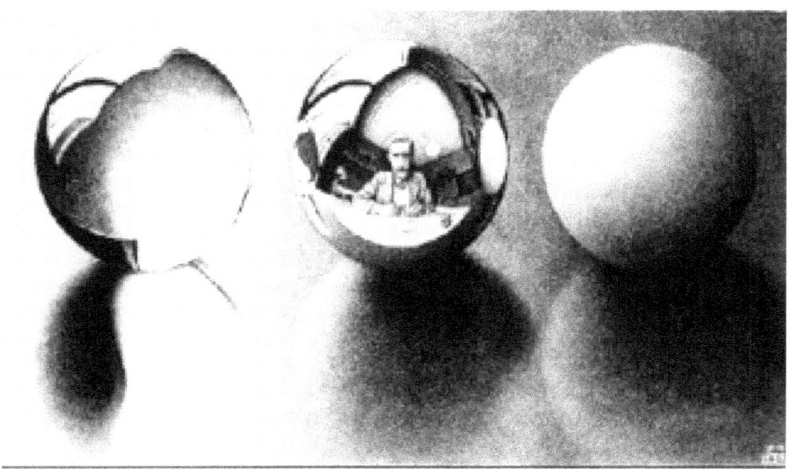

M.C. Escher - Three Spheres

As an example, I have long enjoyed the artwork of M.C. Escher. "Three Spheres" was on the wall above my desk for many years, and the t-shirt I am wearing in the Arizona desert, shown in Chapter 15, features one of Escher's works. So, I knew both his work and appearance fairly well. Around 2013 I saw the work of a young Scandinavian artist, and it reminded me of Escher. However, when I saw his picture, his face also reminded me of Escher, and in that moment I knew he was the reincarnation of Escher.

In the next session with Kevin, Ahtun Re confirmed that this young artist had indeed been Escher. So, I contacted Walter and told him the story. He expressed interest in contacting the young artist, and wanted to post the case on his site, so I forwarded examples showing the similarities of both artists work. While the Escher case never appeared on his site, it was another example of why some people show highly developed talents at a young age. They have had many lifetimes to develop those talents.

AHTUN RE

Taharqa Pharoah

Kevin works with a few different spirit guides, but the guide that showed up for all of our sessions is named Ahtun Re[59]. He was an Egyptian Priest who lived during the time of Akhenaten[64], the 18th dynasty Pharaoh who built the city of Akhetaten. Ahtun Re was of Nubian descent, and was a master architect of the city of Akhetaten.

When Kevin goes into the trance state, his voice and mannerisms change completely. This can be seen in the movie *Out on a Limb*, where he plays himself, and channels the guides John and Tom McPherson.

The voice of Ahtun Re is similar to the voice of James Earl Jones, deep and commanding. And according to Kevin, his appearance would have been similar to Taharqa, a Nubian Pharaoh from the 25th Dynasty.

According to Ahtun Re, I also had an incarnation during the time of Akhenaten, and he confirmed that we knew each other in that life. Interestingly, both Walter and Kevin also had lifetimes during that period, and both knew Ahtun. According to Kevin, a small but significant percentage of the people who have had sessions with him, knew one of his spirit guides in a previous incarnation.

The one thing that is most consistent during all of the conversations with Ahtun Re, is his compassion and understanding towards people. He does appear to have opinions, but no matter how frustrated I may be with a person or historical event, he always finds a more optimistic and neutral way of framing the situation. In the end, holding grudges and carrying animosity with us to our death only hurts us.

IN THE ETERNAL ⇆

This book, and those that will follow, are not attempting to prove that reincarnation exists. In my view, between the work of Dr. Stevenson and Dr. Semkiw, there is now enough evidence to settle that question. And, most people on the planet already accept the concept, however poorly understood it may be. We are simply wanting to share our story, with the hope that it will contribute to the increasing awareness of the phenomena.

Walter hoped that the awareness of reincarnation as a universal principle of life would help us move beyond our tendency of creating conflict with people of different origin. Here are a few quotes from Walter's site:

> *"As reincarnation research shows we can change religion,*
> *nationality and race from one lifetime to another,*
> *evidence of reincarnation will help us transcend*
> *tribal mindset and bring greater world peace."*

> *"What will end these endless cycles of*
> *violence? Evidence of reincarnation will."*

> *"We fight over cultural markers of identity, though in*
> *truth we are all the same, we are all of one family."*

While it may take a little longer to get to the point where these principles are part of our collective cultures, we are eternal consciousness in human form, so there is plenty of time. I believe we will get there, eventually. It's up to us.

Seann Aswell
Maricopa County, Arizona
April 2023

REFERENCES

135. [image]

Guangxu Emperor

intheeternal.com/en/id/473

136. [Photo]

Seann - 1999 (Dallas, Texas)

intheeternal.com/en/id/477

137. [Note]

Walter Semkiw, MD : About

intheeternal.com/en/id/590

138. [Book]

Walter Semkiw, M. (2008) Origin of the Soul

intheeternal.com/en/id/807

139. [Image]

Adams-Semkiw

intheeternal.com/en/id/606

140. [Link]

Ian Stevenson : Reincarnation Research website

intheeternal.com/en/id/626

13. [Note]

Kevin Ryerson : About

intheeternal.com/en/id/589

141.
[Link]

Reincarnation Research : Core Cases

intheeternal.com/en/id/628

142.
[Image]

Three Spheres

intheeternal.com/en/id/691

143.
[Image]

Taharqa

intheeternal.com/en/id/749

59.
[Note]

Ahtun Re : About

intheeternal.com/en/id/637

64.
[Link]

Akhenaten : Egyptian Pharaoh

intheeternal.com/en/id/634

Sara's Way

"Sara's way" is a meditation technique created by the author of this book. It was developed by combining both independent research and teachings from HeartMath[144].

HeartMath Institute, located in Boulder Creek, California, is known for it's research into 'Heart Intelligence' and the heart-brain connection. The following graph is a comparison of the signals between the heart and the brain in two opposite emotions: the 'negative' emotion of frustration and the 'positive' emotion of appreciation. It clearly shows that frustration generates chaotic rhythms, while appreciation generates harmonic rhythms.

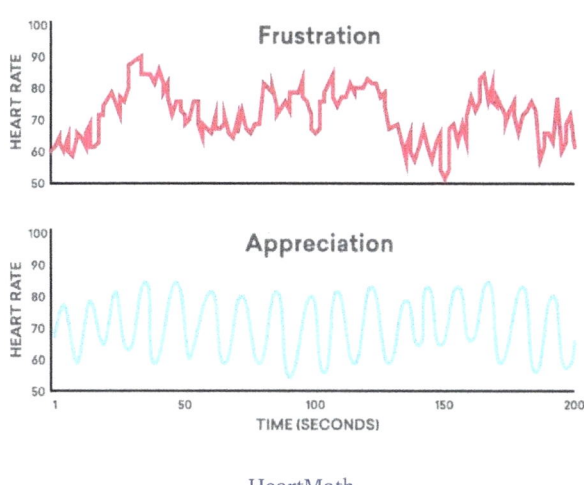

HeartMath

Since 1991, the HeartMath Institute has researched and developed reliable, scientifically based tools that bridge the connection between heart and mind and deepen our connection with the hearts of others. This empowers people to greatly reduce stress, increase resilience, and unlock natural intuitive guidance for making better choices.

Alan Cohen stated in his book *The Dragon Doesn't Live here Anymore*, "when we cultivate the higher emotions of joy, peacefulness, appreciation, devotion, and enthusiasm, we lift ourselves up on the magic carpet of the accumulated thoughts and deeds of all who have ever loved goodness and loving kindness. As we open our arms in appreciation, we are blessed by a power greater than that of our seemingly small action."

The basic principle for this meditation is, we attract whatever we focus on into our reality. If we want peace and happiness, we need to focus on being happy and at peace. The meditation can be practiced sitting or lying down, whatever is comfortable depending on your circumstances. A quiet and secluded space is beneficial, as is soothing or relaxing music, but neither is necessary.

Instructions for the meditation are as follows:

1. Close your eyes, put your hand on your heart (one hand, two hands at your own discretion).

2. Take three deep breaths, 1————, 2————, 3————, as slow as you can.

3. Slowly relax into your normal comfortable breathing pattern.

4. Now, think of a moment in your life where you were feeling joyful. Maybe it was your 5 year old daughter with rosy cheeks and a big smile, holding ice cream in her hand and saying, "mommy, life is good, huh!" Or, maybe you were sailing under the sun, gentle and warm breeze caressing you face, blowing your hair... Or, maybe you're holding hands with the love of your life, strolling on the beach...Or, maybe you're scuba diving and seeing the beauty of a new world for the first time... Or, maybe just simply sitting on your front porch, watching the kids and dogs play... Just find a moment and remember how

you were feeling. Remember the feeling... then, you can let the people, the theme fade away... Just simply feel...... feel the feeling of joy and peace. Keep that feeling in your heart...... and let everything else go......

5. If you find your mind drifting away, just take a deep breath and gently bring your attention back to your heart and continue or stop when you feel the sense of completion.

"Sara's way" is meant to be a short meditation, but it can be practiced repeatedly each day. Once you practice enough, you can jump right into the joyful feelings in your heart, and skip the steps intended to remind you of those feelings.

I call this simple meditation exercise "Sara's way" for my own convenience. You are free to call it anything you'd like. Feel free to modify it in any way that suits you, and feel free to share with anyone that can benefit from it.

Sara Chou
Nevada County, California
March, 2012

REFERENCES

144.   [Link]

HeartMath Institute : website

intheeternal.com/en/id/800

Index